This bird's-eye view of Fredericksburg, painted in 1856, is bordered with depictions of historic sites and structures. Lithograph by E. Sachse Company of Baltimore, Maryland. Courtesy of Historic Urban Plans, Inc. of Ithaca, N.Y.

EDERICKSBURG.

House of Mrs. Washington
in 1782

Dam of the Fredericksburg Water Power Company.
(Rappahannock River)

Presbyterian Church.

Protestant Episcopal Church.

RICKSBURG, VA.

Bo Baltimore Md

IN THE PATH OF HISTORY

Virginia Between the Rappahannock and the Potomac:
An Historical Portrait

By

Nan Netherton
Ruth Preston Rose
Ross Netherton

Published by

Higher Education Publications, Inc., Falls Church, Virginia

ISBN #: 0-914927-46-9

Library of Congress Cataloging-in-Publication Data

Netherton, Nan.
  In the path of history : Virginia between the Rappahannock and the Potomac : an historical portrait / by Nan Netherton, Ruth Preston Rose & Ross Netherton.
      p. cm.
  Includes index.
  ISBN 0-914927-46-9 (alk. paper)
  1. Virginia—History, Local. 2. Rappahannock River Valley (Va.)—History, Local. 3. Potomac River Valley—History, Local. 4. Virginia—History, Local—Pictorial works. 5. Rappahannock River Valley (Va.)—History, Local—Pictorial works. 6. Potomac River Valley—History, Local—Pictorial works. I. Rose, Ruth Preston. II. Netherton, Ross De Witt, 1918- III. Title.
  F232.A15N47 2004
  975.5'044—dc22
                    2004026210

Published by:
Higher Education Publications, Inc.
6400 Arlington Boulevard
Suite 648
Falls Church, Virginia 22042-2336
(703) 532-2300
info@hepinc.com

Contents

Acknowledgements

The three authors are indebted to the following individuals for their reading and constructive comments on the several sections of this book: Mrs. Rexford D. Beckwith III (Miriam J.), Executive Director, Foundation for Historic Christ Church; John C. Wilson, author of *Virginia's Northern Neck*; Barbara Willis, Fredericksburg historian; Jane Sullivan, Thomas Balch Library, Leesburg; Edith Moore Sprouse, Fairfax County History Commission; Thomas M. Moncure, Jr., Clerk of the Court, Stafford County; Dr. Stewart Jones, Stafford County historian; Sara Collins, Arlington Public Library; John Gott, Fauquier County historian; Kim Holien, historian, Fort Myer Military Community and T. Michael Miller, co-author of Alexandria's *Seaport Saga*.

Other interested individuals assisted us with information and images. They included Justin Oosthuizen and Gloria Matthews; Joanna D. Caton and Summer Rutherford, Belmont, the Gari Melchers Estate; C. Vaughan Stanley and Catherine J. Farley, Stratford Hall; Linda Leazer, Virginia Historical Society; Joseph S. White III and Trent M. Park, Virginia Department of Historic Resources; Bradley Gernand, Falls Church historian and archivist; Laura Dutton, Loudoun Museum, Inc.; Richard J. Johnson, editor, Fauquier *Times-Democrat*; Dale Connelly and Sharon Culley, National Archives; staff of Washingtoniana Collection, Martin Luther King, Jr. D. C. Public Library; Suzanne Levy, Anita Ramos, Brian Conley and Karen Moore, Virginia Room, Fairfax County Public Library; Judy Knudsen and Ingrid Kauffman of the Virginia Room of the Arlington County Public Library; Wanda Dowell and Susan Cumby, Fort Ward; Don Wilson, Prince William County Public Library; Douglas Harvey, Scott Harris and Melinda Herzog, Manassas Museum System; Nina F. Carneal, Caledon Natural Area; Carol Ann Cohen and Keith Tomlinson, Northern Virginia Regional Park Authority; Emily Kangas, Gunston Hall; Dawn Bonner, Mount Vernon; and Richard A. Horwege, senior editor, The Donning Company. The postcard collection of Tony Chavez was extensively used.

Special visual contributions were made by artists Ellen Jones, Jackie Cawley, Gloria Matthews, and Helen Ulan and by photographers Warren Mattox, Scott Boatright, Evan Cantrell and Richard Netherton.

A special relationship existed between Nan Netherton and Frederick Hafner, founder of Higher Education Publications, as a result of the publisher's handling of many of Nan's books over her years of writing. "Fritz" Hafner and his staff of editors and designers were her trusted advisors on the wide range of problems that inevitably arise in publishing, and the decisive moment which made possible the publication of *In The Path Of History* was when Hafner offered to continue on as the authors' advisor and the book publisher. To the authors this was a contribution born of mutual respect and lasting friendship, and is acknowledged with deepest thanks. Mark Schreiber of Higher Education Publications expertly designed and typeset the book.

Carol and David Dunlap were our invaluable experts on preparing the book's manuscript for the publisher.

Nan Netherton
Ruth Preston Rose
Ross Netherton

Dedication

This book is dedicated to Nan Netherton, who first saw the need for it, who planned and researched it, who persuaded numerous historians, archivists and librarians to help locate the needed graphics and interpretive information, and whose contagious enthusiasm over a period of more than a decade sustained her colleagues in the thought that this book could indeed be completed in publishable form. In the end she did not live to see the completion of the work she began. It was something she very much wanted and was actively working on up to the time of her death.

In finishing this work we are pleased to dedicate it to Nan, for it really is her book. We hope it reflects both her commitment to history and her enjoyment of the study of history.

In its 2004 session, the Virginia General Assembly adopted a joint resolution recognizing Nan's career in history. The resolution read in part:

WHEREAS Ann Rohrke "Nan" Netherton of Arlington, an award-winning chronicler of the history of Northern Virginia's towns, cities, counties and communities, died on June 9, 2003... [and] for more than half a century she worked tirelessly and with great effectiveness to describe and preserve the rapidly changing Northern Virginia region.

NOW THEREFORE BE IT RESOLVED... That the General Assembly hereby note with great sadness the loss of an exceptional Virginian... and that the Clerk of the Senate prepare a copy of this resolution for presentation... as an expression of the respect in which her memory is held by the members of the General Assembly.

Adopted by the Senate, January 22, 2004;
Agreed to by the House of Delegates, January 30, 2004

Ruth Preston Rose
Ross Netherton

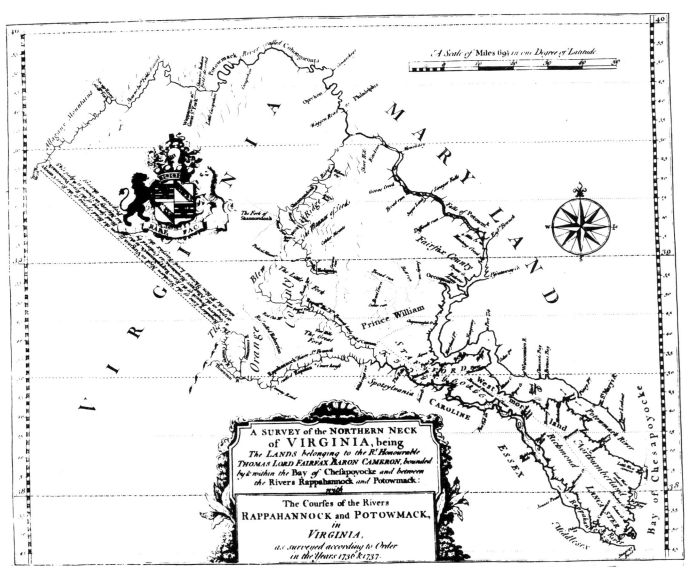

The Northern Neck Proprietary, as surveyed in 1737 in connection with confirmation of Thomas Lord Fairfax as royal Proprietor. Although the land grant extended from Chesapeake Bay to the headsprings of the Potomac and Rappahannock Rivers, the land west of the Blue Ridge had very few settlers and at the time had not been surveyed or mapped.

I

Proprietors of the Northern Neck

The natural bounty and beauty of Chesapeake Bay and its adjacent areas was first described in glowing terms by Captain John Smith when he explored the bay and its tributaries. In his book about this journey, *The Generall Historie of Virginia . . .*, published in 1624, he wrote, in part: "Heaven & earth never agreed better to frame a place for man's habitation; were it fully manured and inhabited by industrious people. Here are mountaines, hils, plaines, valleyes, rivers, and brookes, all running most pleasantly into a fair Bay, compassed but for the mouth, with fruitfull and delightsome land."

In the late 1500s and the early 1600s, Virginia seemed like a cornucopia of plenty. Smith and other writers left lists of the many things which combined to describe a virtual Garden of Eden in the then accessible parts of the colony. Wild deer, geese, cranes, ducks, swans and herons abounded. Many varieties of fish swam in abundance in the rivers and the bay. Crabs and oysters were plentiful. On land the Native American residents planted and harvested crops of corn, potatoes, pumpkins, onions, peas, beans and tobacco. These reports made up the view of Virginia carried by English settlers who followed the Jamestown expedition.

In contrast, by the mid-1600s England was in chaos. During Oliver Cromwell's Commonwealth, the heir to the throne, Charles II, fled into exile in France. There, in gratitude to seven loyal followers who went with him, in 1649 he granted to them all of the land between the Rappahannock and Potomac rivers in the colony of Virginia, an area known popularly as The Northern Neck Proprietary.

After the death of Cromwell in 1658, Charles II was restored to the throne of England, and subsequently arranged to put the Northern Neck Proprietary Grant into effect. By that time, Thomas, 2nd Lord Culpeper, Baron of Thoresway, and Thomas, 5th Baron of Cameron, had acquired the interests of the original grantees. When Lord Culpeper died in 1689, he left the proprietary to his only legitimate heir, his daughter Catherine. The following year, she married Thomas, 5th Lord Fairfax, and by the law of the time he then became owner of his wife's property, including her share of the proprietary.

Proprietary grants of this sort were made throughout the colonies in the seventeenth century where there was unclaimed or unsettled land. It was a practice traced to the feudal system of creating "manors" or territories held by a lord directly from and under the royal sovereign. Originally its purpose had been to impose and maintain order and loyalty in areas where the sovereign's control was insecure, and by the terms of their patents the proprietors frequently exercised many powers of government and distribution of land.

The circumstances of Virginia in the eighteenth century however made this use of proprietaries impractical, and so the Northern Neck grant was "modified" to give the Royal Governor and General Assembly authority to tax and make laws applicable to the proprietary lands along with the rest of the colony. By the time the Northern Neck Proprietary came to the 6th Lord Fairfax it had become essentially a land-grant. Yet the proprietary duties of maintaining and administering this grant were substantial, and in 1702 Lord Fairfax appointed Robert Carter of Lancaster County as his agent.

Carter proved to be an able agent. A well-educated, ambitious and influential Virginian, he not only collected annual quitrents from the leaseholders, but also defended what he considered to be the boundaries of the then unmapped territory. In 1719, Thomas, 6th Lord Fairfax, inherited the Proprietary, but he came to America only after the Virginia Governor and Council challenged the legitimacy of his proprietary title. To defend his Virginia domain, the 6th Lord Fairfax sought to have it confirmed by the King. In 1733 the Privy Council in London, responding to petitions from Virginia, ordered the boundaries of the proprietary "surveyed and settled" by a joint commission. It was decided that surveyor William Mayo would prepare a map for Virginia's Governor, Sir William Gooch, and that surveyor John Warner would prepare one for Thomas, 6th Lord Fairfax.

By 1737 the two completed maps reached London, where they were studied by the royal authorities for eight more years. In 1745, a committee of the King's Privy Council decided the case by confirming, with few exceptions, the full territory claimed by Fairfax, over 5,000,000 acres in all, based on the John Warner survey.

Hardly were these legal challenges to the Proprietary title overcome, than new threats to settlement arose in its western parts. Up and down the Shenandoah Valley, settlers were subject to raids and depredations of the Indians resisting the invasion of lands which historically had been part of their hunting reserve. After 1750 these raids become more frequent and aggressive as the French colonial administration in Canada equipped and encouraged them to block the efforts of settlers from Virginia, Pennsylvania, New York and the Carolinas to settle west of the Appalachians.

As England and France confronted each other around the world, the Proprietor was expected to defend his lands and its residents with the county militia. This was, of course, an impossible task on the lightly-settled western frontier. Some left the Valley for safer parts, and those who stayed on their land prepared, where possible, to seek refuge in one of the neighborhood's stone "fortified houses" or in settlements large enough to thwart the marauding war-parties.

The level of danger to settlers in the Valley lands was lowered after the French abandonment of Fort Duquesne in 1757 deprived the Indians of their source of supply. Meanwhile, during the British struggle to oust France from North America, crops and cattle from the Northern Neck fed both British and Colonial troops in their campaigns to the north and south of Virginia. Tobacco was also raised, although not of a grade that commanded the best prices, And lack of a network of all-weather roads limited the movement of agricultural products.

When fighting ceased, settlement resumed, and prompted the Proprietor to relocate his land office from the family seat at Belvoir in the Tidewater to Greenway Court in the vicinity of Winchester. Thus at a time when many Tidewater planters carried large burdens of debt to London merchant and banking houses, the Proprietor of the Northern Neck enjoyed a sound financial position by virtue of his life-style, cautious management of his estate, and avoidance of unnecessary risks.

There were other considerations that favored his quiet country life at Greenway Court. As Virginia joined more fully in the war for American Independence, the Commonwealth's Assembly turned to raising needed revenue by measures such as trebling the tax on quitrents. Also, the Assembly passed legislation requiring all free-born males over the age of 16 to take an oath renouncing allegiance to George III. "Recusants" could refuse to take the oath but they would be disqualified from holding any public office, serving on juries, or having access to the courts of Virginia. Personally, and as far as the Northern Neck Proprietary was concerned, Fairfax would have had no difficulty taking this oath. But had he done so the family estates in England, incuding Leeds Castle, might well have been sequestered by the Crown. The risk was too great; and so Fairfax accepted the status of a "recusant" with the added burdens it entailed. In 1777 quitrents were abolished in Virginia, but by that time the growing trade in agricultural produce helped

Thomas Fairfax, Sixth Baron of Cameron, was born at Leeds Castle in Kent, England in 1693. He was the only proprietor to reside in Northern Virginia. The county, established in 1742, was named after him. He administered over 5,200,000 acres of land in Virginia until his death in 1781. Portrait by Joshua Reynolds; courtesy of Alexandria-Washington Lodge No. 22, A.F & A.M., Alexandria, Virginia

By mid-nineteenth century most freight and passenger transportation went by river in the Tidewater communities and by railroad in much of the Piedmont. But a great deal of land was not connected to rail or water transportation by all-weather roads. Carl Rakeman's historical painting of the "Dark Age" of roads illustrates how bad roads isolated rural parts of the region for most of the year and affected patterns of regional development. Source: Federal Highway Administration

offset the loss of quitrent income. In 1779 the Assembly took the further step of distinguishing between citizens of Virginia and citizens whose loyalty was to King George, but an exception was made for Lord Fairfax by reason of his long residence in Virginia, plus the general good feeling and respect he enjoyed throughout the Northern Neck.

Thus the 6th Lord Fairfax passed the rest of his days at Greenway Court, amid surroundings of his own choosing. He died peacefully on December 9, 1781, at the age of 88, and was buried at Winchester, according to contemporary accounts, "with all the decency the present situation of affairs permitted, tho' not in a manner his rank and fortune required."

Writing later, George Washington observed, "altho' the good Lord ... lived to an advanced age, I feel concern at his death." Some of his concern might well have been for the future of the proprietary. Title to the part he had previously inherited from the Culpepers passed under the terms of his Lordship's will to a nephew. But the interest acquired by marriage to Catherine Culpeper passed by operation of law to a cousin in England, Robert, 7th Lord Fairfax, and thus it became subject to the Virginia statute of 1779 declaring that property

belonging to "British subjects" was vested in the Commonwealth.

This effectively ended questions about the future of the Proprietary as a legal entity recognized by Virginia. Thenceforth it shared the fortunes of Virginia, and these were not always as they had been in the past. New personalities would become proprietors "in fact," if not in law between the Rappahannock and the Potomac.

In this regard, by mid-nineteenth century Virginia was noticeably less influential in its own and in the nation's business than it had been as a royal colony. The historian Virginius Dabney attributes this "decline" to several factors: By 1850 large numbers of Virginia's young and most vigorous generation were moving to the newly-opened regions of the West and South; an inefficient system of slave labor discouraged growth of industry generally; archaic primary and secondary educational systems resulted in Virginia ranking 25th out of 31 states in its level of literacy, and began to reduce enrollment in the College of William and Mary.

One feature of this period, however, was generally praised. That was the effort to revive agriculture in the Northern Neck. Introduction of fertilizers, rotation and diversification of crops, deep plowing, manuring, and a switch to growing grain led to reversal of the soil exhaustion and erosion which had prevailed in the era of tobacco. Interest in experimentation and the activities of scientific farming societies were strong in this area. Cultivation of orchards and garden produce for export to urban centers and raising livestock for market helped produce an upturn in the region's agriculture. Indeed, in the 1850s farmers of the Northern Neck were regarded as becoming one of the richest agricultural groups in America, a fact evidenced by the colonies of Northern farmers who settled in the Tidewater counties and in the riverine parts of present-day Fairfax, Loudoun, Stafford and Prince William counties in the 1840s and 1850s.

Beneficial as these advancements in agriculture were, however, it still was clear to Virginians of the 1850s that the competitive advantage they enjoyed in the eighteenth century, and the economic, political and social influence it conferred, could not be readily retrieved in their present circumstances. Much of the lost ground that had to be made up involved development of a transportation infrastructure. In the eighteenth century, transportation was provided by the Potomac and the Rappahannock and their tributaries. And they continued to to be important. But in the early nineteenth century Alexandria and Fredericksburg, located at the limits of navigation, were not well connected to their inland areas by roads or rails. Time would be needed to remedy this competitive disadvantage, and by 1860 time to do so had run out.

Events in the land and waters between the Rappahannock and Potomac Rivers during the years of conflict are described elsewhere. Suffice it to say that probably no other region in America suffered as long and in as many ways as this one did. Unfortunately, when armies became the temporary proprietors of the Northern Neck, everything in the environment and lifestyle of the residents became "expendable for the duration." When the time for reconstruction came, therefore, very little of the pre-war political, economic and social systems could be recognized as holding over or even restorable. Reconstruction after restoration of statehood weighed heavily on local government since the state government was sorely stressed simply to survive. At the local level the framework for governing was new. The old County Court system, inherited from colonial times, was replaced by Boards of Supervisors whose members were elected from Magisterial Districts, and whose functions were political and administrative. Time and effort would be needed to make the new system work.

Much of the vigor needed to rebuild the civilian community was provided by newcomers from New England, the mid-Atlantic states and the mid-West. Some were already acquainted with Northern Virginia from previous military service; others came because post-war conditions where they lived were unattractive. And, of course, there were the speculators and opportunists. In the old Proprietary, however, they became sources of energy, investment capital, new ideas and know-how, and not least, a sense of confidence in themselves and their future prospects. The socio-economic system of the colonial Proprietary, in which planters with large landholdings had been the sources of capital and initiative for investment in such industrial ventures as mills, iron foundries, and shipyards, was gone.

As the new system emerged, the patterns of population growth and development shifted. By the 1880s, the city of Washington had evolved from a provincial town to a cosmopolitan capital. The Federal government had grown in size, and required services on a substantial scale. Farmers and merchants near enough to deliver goods or services into Washington by road or railway found it worthwhile to do so. Surpluses continued to go to more distant markets by water or rail from Washington and Alexandria.

Once again, transportation influenced the pace and direction of growth. Only a few of the turnpikes built prior to 1860 survived, and financial prospects for revival of such road construction were poor. But interest in regional networks of electric railways, popularly called "interurban lines," was high at the turn of the twentieth century, and they provided Alexandria, Arlington and Fairfax County rapid daily transportation for commuters, school children, truck garden and dairy produce, mail and parcel delivery. Heavy freight, even components for home construction from mail order companies, came by steam railroad lines running through Washington and Alexandria to the south and west.

Centers of commerce and industry in colonial times had been at the fall lines of the navigable streams emptying into Chesapeake Bay. Now they moved back into the Piedmont as railroad construction linked riverside shippers with inland sources of supply and markets.

From World War I onward in the twentieth century the easy availability of motor vehicles and the on-going construction of road networks became leading factors in determining where people lived and worked.

Between the first and second World Wars much of the population growth in the National Capital region was absorbed in the District of Columbia and Maryland. But the surge in population and economic activity during and following World War II shifted to Virginia where land was still in farms or open space in the 1950s. In the same decade a massive highway modernization program with Federal-aid financing foreshadowed the domination of American surface transportation by motor vehicles and highways, and passenger travel by air and automobile.

The significance of reshaping the transportation infrastructure in this way became apparent in the last half of the century when the mid-section of the old Proprietary became the seedbed for a series of centers of economic activity. They had the appearance of self-sufficiency with supporting services at hand, all carefully arranged to accommodate highway freight haulers, parking space for thousands of cars, and service facilities for hundreds of stores and hundreds of thousands of square feet of office space. Equally large and complex telecommunications and utilities systems also are there but invisible underground.

When the pattern of local and interregional expressways was overlaid on a map of the old Northern Neck Proprietary, it became a grid for identifying places where development of this type could be undertaken most profitably. Sometimes referred to as "Edge Cities," these places provided the functions that a city performs, but were located well beyond the old downtown central business districts, out on the edges of urban areas. In the 1960s, 1970s and 1980s they became the focal points of land use policy and politics in the old proprietary's counties of Arlington, Fairfax, Prince William and Loudoun.

From this trend emerged a long-standing contradiction in values. Americans believed that "progress" was good—and also that it was inevitable. Thus, they welcomed it and those who brought it. Yet they clung to the conviction that a connection to the land also was good, and that land left (or deliberately kept) in a natural state had a healing effect on the tensions fostered by urbanization. The geographer Jean Gottman commented that "serenity" is the valuable crop harvested from land left in nature's care; or, one might say, if not in the sole care of nature, then in that of a man-made surrogate such as the Northern Virginia Regional Park Authority or similar entity. This contradiction continues to vex the proprietors of the land between the Rappahannock and the Potomac.

This is not a place to judge the merits of natural versus man-made environments, or how an accommodation between them may be devised. Suffice to say only

that the twentieth-century proprietors did not succeed in putting the issue to rest.

Will "Edge Cities" become the trademark of the twenty-first century proprietors of the lands and waters between the Rappahannock and Potomac? And, if this occurs will the area steadily be swallowed by the megalopolis that extends from Boston to Washington, looking ultimately to an anchorage in Norfolk?

These and related questions were noted by the economic geographer Jean Gottman, in his study *Virginia In Our Century*. He warned that "what is happening to northern Virginia and threatening much of the Tidewater is not a simple metropolitan growth explained entirely by the expansion of the national capital's role and size. It is a much bigger and deeper influence:...the extension southward of what could have been called 'the Main Street of the Nation,' already a 'megalopolitan' system some 400 miles long."

Writing in 1969, Gottman did not try to predict the future of the Northern Neck Proprietary, but by calling attention to this trend toward urbanization he could not fail to raise another question, that is: will continued growth of this megalopolis result in obliterating many of the features that have in the past, and still do serve to give the old Proprietary its unique diversity?

Developers who have or who will become the new proprietors of the old Northern Neck Proprietary may see it mainly as one big market area throughout which the services needed by the economy can be provided most efficiently when they are uniform, standardized, interchangeable, and largely identical. And they may view the area's work force as a single, highly mobile labor pool, the members of which can commute daily from any corner of the area to any other. They may foresee that the advanced technology of telecommunications will wipe out the region's villages, towns and cities by taking over one of their most important functions.

These are ideas which, if utilized aggressively for short term advantages, could easily eliminate many of the natural and cultural features which reflect the unique character of the old Proprietary. Many who have grown up with and appreciate this rich diversity will hope that ways can be found to move with the times while preserving the tangible expressions of the region's distinguished place in the path of history.

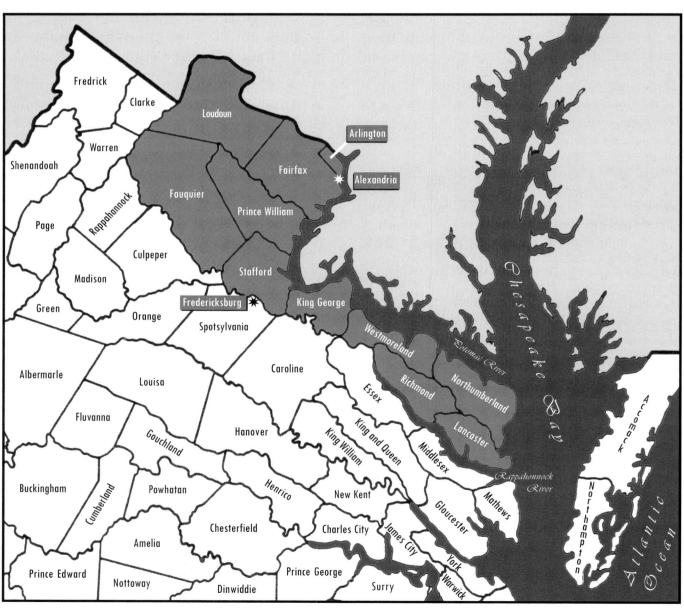

Virginia Counties, 1861-1895. Counties and cities between the Potomac and Rappahonnock rivers featured in this book are highlighted in dark gray.

II

The Early Counties Between
the Rappahannock and Potomac Rivers

European explorers began visiting Virginia's north-ernmost peninsula as early as 1588, when the Spanish captain Vicente Gonzales sailed up Chesapeake Bay and found the area well populated with natives divided into chiefdoms under the control of Chief Powhatan. As English settlers arrived in the next century, relations between the newcomers and the natives were generally good, and an active trade was carried on between the two groups.

John Mottrom, who settled at Coan Hall on the Potomac River, arrived in 1640 and is believed to be the first Englishman to settle on the peninsula. He and other early settlers had crossed the river from Maryland where, as Protestants, they found the atmosphere created by the Royalist governor, Lord Calvert, to be uncongenial with their religious and political thinking. Among other early settlers were the ancestors of two presidents: Andrew Monroe arrived from Maryland in 1648, and John Washington settled in the area a few years later.

Chickacoan, the Algonquin area where John Mottrom settled, became known as Northumberland County in 1645. Three more counties came into being by 1656: Lancaster, Westmoreland and Rappahannock. A portion of Rappahannock County later became Richmond County, and King George County was formed in 1721 as settlers moved westward.

As the counties of the peninsula became more densely populated with Englishmen, the native population was diminished until most of them had moved away or become mingled with settlers. Only one group of natives remained into the 20th century.

Parishes were created in the newly-settled areas, with vestries appointed to levy taxes and assessments, while churchwardens were assigned the control of moral behavior of the parishioners. A statute of 1642-43 charged the vestrymen with conducting surveys, directing the building and repairing of bridges and the clearing of roads, duties in which the men of the parish were required to participate. Vestrymen also were charged with the care of orphans and the poor. As leading men of the community, vestrymen became magistrates, members of the colony's governing body, and, in the 18th century, leaders of the revolution which resulted in the formation of the United States. Justices were appointed by the General Council at Jamestown; and during the early years of settlement when many counties lacked courthouses, their courts' monthly sessions often met at the homes of members of the court.

The introduction of slavery enabled wealthier families to establish large plantations along the rivers where quantities of tobacco could be grown and shipped, while less affluent families settled on smaller inland farms. Industries related to fishing and forest products originated in colonial times, but the area's rural character has continued into the 21st century.

Today the contributions made by the peninsula counties in creating the institutions of Virginia's colonial economy and civil government can be revisited in old churches, warehouses, barns and farmsteads, courthouses and other public buildings which survive. Preservation of many of these places has been aided in part by their relative isolation from the forces that have favored industrial and commercial development elsewhere. While these forces fostered the rise of urban centers at inland locations, the peninsular counties have continued to serve as sources of fishing and forest products, and have been bypassed by the major transportation systems that encouraged development of towns and commercial centers elsewhere.

Amoung the boats used for bringing menhaden fish to the factories along the coast were these early 20th century wooden-hulled boats at Menhaden Products, Inc. at Fleeton, in Northumberland County. The McKeever Brothers, *right, was converted into a restaurant.* Courtesy of Isabel Gough and John C. Wilson

Northumberland County

Northumberland County was mentioned in the records of the "Grand Assembly holden att James City" in February of 1645, when it was decreed that the inhabitants of the county were expected to "wholly contribute towards the maintenance of the warr" against the Indians. In 1648, the tract of land between the Rappahannock and Potomac rivers was officially named Northumberland.

The Englishmen who came to the Northern Neck in the 1640s found the land along the rivers populated with Indians who lived in villages surrounded by cultivated fields, as John Smith had observed them in his 1608 exploration. Archaeological excavations have indicated that Indians lived on the peninsula for several thousand years. Numerous Indian names remain in Northumberland and in other parts of the peninsula, in geographic locations, in the names of houses, and in church designations. Soon after the formation of the county, the parish of Great Wiccocomoco, named for a local Indian district, was established, and a church was built near the site of the present Wicomico Episcopal Church.

English settlers in the county included Richard Lee who had settled on Dividing Creek by 1651 when he represented the county in the colony's legislature. In 1652, he petitioned for a free school in the Cobbs Hall area. Lee died in 1664, leaving a large estate, including the land left to his son Hancock, where Ditchley was later built. Another early settler, Captain William Ball, Jr., son of the immigrant, lived at Ball's Neck. He surveyed the boundary line between Northumberland and Lancaster counties in 1686.

The wealthier settlers on the Northern Neck obtained large land holdings along the waterways, for the rivers provided the primary means of communication with other parts of the world. Besides transportation, the water gave the settlers a large portion of their food because of the abundant supply of fish and water fowl. Most families lived in small, vernacular houses that have not survived.

The large mansions for which the area is known followed the introduction of slavery that made it possible for sufficient production of goods, especially tobacco, to support a grand lifestyle.

The waterways continued to be the most important means of transportation in the nineteenth century, when steamboats carried most Northumberland traffic in both passengers and goods. Entertainment also could be found on the water in the form of theater boats. A memorable floating theater was the *James Adams*, which plied the waters in the early twentieth century.

Although lacking military engagements, Northumberland has not been without war heroes. Among them were three members of the family of Colonel Thomas Jones of Mount Zion near present-day Callao. Twin sons, Thomas ap Catesby Jones and Roger Jones had distinguished careers in the military spanning the War of 1812 and the Mexican War. Catesby ap Roger Jones is remembered for outfitting the *Merrimac*, which became the Confederate Navy's ironclad *Virginia*, for its battle with the *Monitor*, during which Jones was commander of the ship. Another military leader connected with the county was General Zachary Taylor, the twelfth president of the United States. He was descended from the Ditchley Lees through his grandmother, Elizabeth, a daughter of Hancock Lee (1653-1709.)

Although Northumberland County had a history of free schools from the time of Richard Lee, the immigrant, general education was largely unavailable until after the Civil War, when the Reconstruction Constitution mandated public schools in the entire state. Several private schools were formed for the children of freedmen, among them Howland Chapel School, established by New York philanthropist Emily Howland in 1867, and the Holley School, started by Sallie Holley in 1868.

The population of Northumberland County in 1790 was 9,103; and in 2000 was 12,259, indicating the continuing rural character of the area.

Heathsville Historic District includes the courthouse, which was constructed in 1851 to serve Northumberland County residents. Heathsville has been the county seat since 1681, and was originally known as Hughlett's Tavern. Besides the courthouse and the tavern, Heathsville Historic District includes an unusual Civil War memorial, a brick Methodist church with classical features, and other notable buildings. Heathsville was named for John Heath (1761–1810), who was an organizer of Phi Beta Kappa while a student at the College of William and Mary and was the fraternity's first president.
Courtesy of Northumberland County

St. Stephens Episcopal Church in Heathsville was designed around 1881 by Baltimore architect T. Buckler Chequiere. Formed in 1698, St. Stephen's Parish suffered from loss of support following abolition of the established church after the Revolution, when other denominations, especially the Baptists and Presbyterians, gained strength. St. Stephen's Parish was reactivated by the Episcopal Church in 1824. Photograph by J. M. O'Dell, courtesy of the Virginia Department of Historic Resources

Hughlett's Tavern, or Rice's Hotel, started as a two-room tavern in the middle of the 18th century and gave the surrounding community its name. Over time, the tavern grew to its present length of 110 feet. In 1866, John Rice acquired the tavern, and the Rice family operated their hotel until the 1920s. Eventually the building was donated to the Northumberland County Historical Society by Cecilia Fallin Rice. With the formation of the Rice's Hotel/Hughlett Tavern Foundation, restoration of the property was begun under the leadership of Martha Robinson. Courtesy of the Virginia Department of Historic Resources

Constructed in the mid-1700s by Kendall Lee, Ditchley stands on land patented in 1651 by Richard Lee, the immigrant, who was in turn Attorney General, Secretary of State, and a member of the King's Council. He settled on Dividing Creek in 1678. During most of the 19th century the house was owned by the Ball family. In 1932 it was purchased by Mr. and Mrs. Alfred I. duPont. Photograph by C. O. Green, courtesy of the Library of Congress

Jessie Dew Ball duPont was born at Cressfield on Ball's Point in 1884. Her ancestry extended far back into the history of Virginia, for the Balls were among the early settlers in the Northern Neck. Mrs. duPont and her husband, Alfred Irenee duPont, divided their time between Nemours, near Wilmington, Delaware, and Ditchley. Mr. duPont died in 1935; his wife continued her charitable enterprises throughout her life, which ended in 1970. She was a benefactor and director of the Robert E. Lee Memorial Association, formed in 1929 to save Stratford Hall. Its library is named in her honor. She was benefactor of numerous libraries throughout the United States. Her philanthropies continue through the Jessie Ball duPont Religious, Charitable, and Educational Fund. Photo courtesy of Jessie Ball duPont Library, Stratford Hall Plantation, and John C. Wilson

Born in 1827, Elijah W. Reed became a sailor at the age of eighteen and by the age of thirty-one was captain of the Laura Campbell, *a commercial barque owned by a New York Company. Reed commanded the three-masted square-rigged vessel on voyages to England, South America and other ports until he contracted yellow fever in 1863. He emigrated to Virginia in 1867, building a menhaden factory on Cockrell's Creek. A marble obelisk in the center of town is dedicated to the man for whom Reedville was named. The portrait of Captain Elijah W. Reed hangs in the Fishermen's Museum.* Courtesy of W. Reed Randolph

This brick house was built on the main street of Reedville by Captain James C. Fisher and is called The Gables. Captain Fisher owned one of the menhaden factories in Reedville. The main street of Reedville was formerly known as "Millionaires' Row" because of the number of large houses belonging to sea captains. The Gables is in the Reedville Historic District. Courtesy of Dr. and Mrs. Norman Clark

The Reedville Fishermen's Museum, opened in 1990, is housed in the William Walker House, erected before 1875. A grant from the Virginia General Assembly in 1988 enabled the local community to restore the house for use as a museum. In 1995, a large addition was built following a generous gift to the museum by Mr. Frank Covington. Although the abundance of fish was noted by Captain John Smith, it was not until after the Civil War that menhaden fishing became a lucrative industry in the area. Photograph by Ruth P. Rose

In this 1930s photograph, fishermen are shown in one of two boats used to haul in a seine filled with menhaden fish, which travel in dense schools that are readily caught up in the manner shown. Naturalist Mark Catesby recorded in the eighteenth century that large numbers of the fish would wash ashore, and that residents would pick up as many as they needed. Courtesy of Meredith Robbins and John C. Wilson

Shown at Kinsale wharf, the steamship Northumberland *was built in 1900 for the Potomac River route of the Weems Line, begun by the Weems family of Maryland in the early 19th century. Steamboats plied the length of the Chesapeake Bay from the mouth of the Susquehanna River to the mouth of the bay.*

When author Charles Dickens took a steamer from Washington in 1842, he slept in the gentlemen's cabin with more than forty other men, getting under way at dawn. The passengers disembarked at Potomac Creek, got aboard stagecoaches, and traveled ten miles to Fredericksburg, where they boarded a train to Richmond. Courtesy of Ben Franklin, William Franklin and John C. Wilson

Torn down in 1967, the Great Wicomico Light was the last of the old screwpile lighthouses in the Chesapeake Bay. It was constructed in 1889 and was also known as Fleeton Point Light and Gough's Bar Light. Similar lighthouses stood at Smith's Point and at Windmill Point. They have been replaced by automated, galvanized steel towers. Men at sea regarded the keepers of lights with reverence for their diligence in carrying out their lonely tasks. Courtesy of the U. S. Coast Guard and John C. Wilson

Lancaster County

Lancaster County was formed in 1651, and in 1654 two parishes were formed in the county, which at the time lay on both sides of the Rappahannock River. Early parish officials were men who also were members of the county court. Among that number was John Carter, a member of the King's Council and father of Robert "King" Carter. John Carter built the first Christ Church, and his remains have been placed in the present structure. England's Act of Union in 1707 encouraged Scottish traders and factors to settle in Northern Virginia.

The seat of Lancaster County since the 1740s has been Lancaster Court House, now an historic district that includes the courthouse, an 18th century clerk's office, a tavern, the old jail, and other historic buildings. In the archives are records which go back as early as 1652, when the will of Epraphrodibus Lawson was recorded.

In the 18th century court records of the county, one may learn of the punishment given for individuals convicted of crimes such as dancing or fishing on Sunday, speaking profanity, or having fatherless children, for which the culprit might sit in the pillory or suffer lashes to the bare back. A convicted burglar might be transported out of the colony, and thieves often had their ears nailed to the pillory, followed by mutilation–specifically, the ears were cut off.

A study of land ownership in 18th century Lancaster County has shown that sixty to seventy percent of landowners had 200 acres or less, while only one person owned more than 2,000 acres, and many residents owned no land at all. The contrast with the popular idea of southern plantation life in colonial Virginia is striking. In 1790, Lancaster County had a population of 5,638. The census for 2000 showed a population of 11,567.

The 18th Century jail and the 1797 brick clerk's office are at the center of the Lancaster Courthouse Historic District. Established as the county seat in 1740, the historic district includes an 1884 Carpenters' Gothic church (Trinity Episcopal), a c. 1800 tavern, a store, and the Mary Ball Washington Museum. Carolyn H. Jett photos, © 2004, all rights reserved. Used with permission.

St. Mary's Whitechapel is one of the churches of Christ Church Parish, formed in 1668. The oldest gravestone bears the epitaph, "Here lieth interred the body of John Stretchley, Gentleman, who died in 1648." An exceptionally fine iron fence surrounds the graves of members of the Rock family. Raised stones in the foreground mark graves of members of the Ball family. Still in possession of St. Mary's Whitechapel are the chalice, given by David Fox, Sr. in 1669, and the paten given by George Spencer in 1690. Photograph by Ruth P. Rose

Born in 1663 at his father's house at Corotoman in Lancaster County, Robert "King" Carter inherited a large estate from his father. He was educated in England and eventually held every important political office in the colony, including president of the Governor's Council and acting Governor. He also served as agent for Lord Fairfax's Northern Neck Proprietary. Among his descendants were two presidents of the United States (the Harrisons), three signers of the Declaration of Independence (Carter Braxton, Thomas Nelson, and Benjamin Harrison), and Confederate General Robert E. Lee. Courtesy of the National Portrait Gallery of the Smithsonian Institution

Built in classical style with soaring brick walls and roof of unusually steep pitch and sharply splayed eaves, Christ Church has long been recognized as one of the great buildings of colonial Virginia. Geometrical in form and built in a cruciform plan, the church appears to have been the work of a professional architect, although none has been identified. Proposed and built by Robert "King" Carter to replace a 1670 church built by his father, John, Christ Church was erected in 1732-1735. Of the arched ceiling and triple-tiered pulpit, Bishop William Meade wrote that the arrangement seemed "to give force and music to the feeblest tongue." (Clark, Colonial Churches) *Christ Church is used for regular services during the summer months.* Courtesy of the Foundation for Historic Christ Church

The original communion silver at Christ Church was made in London. The service includes the bason, made in 1695-6, the flagon, probably made by Thomas Folkingham in 1720-21, and the chalice and paten cover, which were made around 1681-82. The Christ Church parish silver is displayed at the church's Bierne Carter Museum. Courtesy of the Foundation for Historic Christ Church

Lewis Lunsford began to preach in Westmoreland around 1774, organizing the Morattico Baptist Church soon afterwards. The present structure was erected in 1856. Meeting with considerable opposition, sometimes violence, Lunsford was aided by Councillor Robert Carter of Nomini Hall, who converted to the Baptist faith. A notable Baptist representative of Morattico Church was Henrietta Hall Shuck, who became a missionary to China in 1836. Courtesy of the photographer, John C. Wilson

The Tides Inn, located on Carter's Creek at Irvington, is one of the foremost hotels and resort complexes in the United States. Guests may enjoy golfing, boating, or sightseeing in the historic Northern Neck peninsula. Constructed on the former Ashburn Farm, The Tides Inn was opened in 1947 by Mr. and Mrs. E. A. Stephens. Cypress paneling came from a nearby swamp and was hauled by oxen to the local sawmill. Separately owned, at the far eastern tip of the peninsula, where the Rappahannock River meets the Chesapeake Bay, the Windmill Point Resort, Conference, and Yachting Center is located, where 150 ships have direct access to the bay. Courtesy of The Tides Inn

Incorporated in 1930, Kilmarnock was built at a crossroads on land that was patented by Gervase Dodson and George Wale in the 17th century. In 1676, Anthony Steptoe, who came to Virginia as an indentured servant, purchased 278 acres of the land at the crossroads. His son John, who married a daughter of Hancock Lee, kept a tavern at the crossroads. Photograph by W. A. Haslip. Courtesy of the Kilmarnock Museum

Westmoreland County

During the decade following the arrival in the 1640s of English settlers on the Northern Neck, population increased so rapidly that in July of 1653, the Grand Assembly ordered that a new county be established in the vast territory of the western part of the peninsula. A number of other counties would later be carved from this large area.

Among the early settlers in Westmoreland County were forebears of Presidents George Washington, James Monroe, and Zachary Taylor. Another early settler was Richard Lee, the progenitor of the distinguished family which produced two signers of the Declaration of Independence and the Confederate leader, General Robert E. Lee. Also in the family was Thomas Lee, builder of Stratford Hall and father of Francis Lightfoot Lee, William Lee, Arthur Lee and Richard Henry Lee, all of whom played important roles in the revolutionary years.

Although Westmoreland throughout its history has been primarily an agricultural county, there were some industries active in the 18th century. The Bristol Iron Works, operated by John Lomax, John Tayloe, and Augustine Washington, was active from 1721 to 1729. The Walter Jones Kiln was established by a Welsh potter in 1677 and operated for a short time. Fragments of Jones's pottery have been found at Wakefield, Stratford, and Nominy Plantation.

As early as 1700, there was a free school in Westmoreland County, endowed by William Horton, but, as in other Virginia counties, only those children who could afford private schooling were likely to receive an education until after the Civil War.

In 1790, there were 7,722 residents in the county, 4,425 of them slaves. In 2000, there was a total of 16,718 residents.

The columned portico was added to the Westmoreland County Courthouse in the 1930s. Captured by the British in 1814, the building was begun in 1707 on the site where a courthouse has stood since 1669. Montross, the county seat, was named by an act of incorporation as the town of "Mont Ross" in 1852. Courtesy of the National Archives

Monrovia, the birthplace in 1758 of President James Monroe, was located near Mattox Creek. An obelisk now marks the spot where the house stood on land patented by the Scotsman, Andrew Monroe, who was banished from England because of his role in the Battle of Preston. He patented land on the Potomac in 1650, and became a leading member of the community. Archaeological excavation of the house site in 1976 revealed a structure much as it appears in this drawing from Robert Sears' The Pictorial Description of the American Revolution *(1845).*

A drawing by Benson Lossing shows Wakefield, the birthplace of George Washington in Westmoreland County. Formerly known as Pope's Creek, the estate was purchased in 1717 or 1718 by Augustine Washington, who built the house for himself and his second wife, Mary Ball. After the house burned on Christmas Day 1779, the site fell into decay. The present brick house was built by the Wakefield National Memorial Association, which was incorporated in 1924 under the leadership of Mrs. Josephine Wheelright Rust. From Mount Vernon and Its Associations by Benson Lossing (1859).

A congregation for Yeocomico church of Cople Parish existed as early as 1655, and the building shown was erected in 1706. The varying patterns of brickwork and other architectural features are illustrative of both medieval and Georgian church styles. Used to house soldiers during three wars, Yeocomico is the only colonial church in Westmoreland County. Photograph by Thomas T. Waterman, courtesy of the Library of Congress

In 1790, the largest room at Stratford was described by Thomas Lee Shippen, a grandson of Thomas Lee, the builder: "What a delightful occupation did it afford me, sitting on one of the sofas of the great hall, to trace the family resemblance in the portraits of all my dear mother's forefathers, her father and mother, her grandfather and grandmother, and so on upward for four generations. . . ." The room had no source of heat, so winter balls were probably very lively affairs. Tutor Philip Fithian reported that he attended a ball at Stratford where there was dancing as well as gambling and drinking in the rooms around the hall. Photograph by Jack E. Boucher. Courtesy of the Library of Congress

Richard Henry Lee, the third son of Thomas and Hannah Lee of Stratford, formed the association of patriots who adopted the resolutions known as the Leedstown Association Resolutions in 1766, following the British Stamp Act. At a convention in 1774, Richard Henry Lee was chosen to be one of the six Virginia delegates to the Continental Congress. On June 7, 1776, he introduced a resolution calling for a declaration of independence by the colonies. He signed the subsequent declaration, and he was elected president of the Continental Congress in 1784. His home was Chantilly, on the Potomac, now an archeological site. Courtesy of the Library of Congress

Kinsale was established as an official British port in 1708 at "Yohocomeco upon the land of Richard Tidwell." Burned by the British in 1814, the port revived to become a significant center for smuggling activities during the Civil War. The Bailey family, who own Great House, began placing lights in one of its windows in 1750 as a warning to passing ships. Kinsale has a museum detailing the port's history. Courtesy of the Library of Virginia

The steamer Potomac *is shown in the 1930s at the Colonial Beach pier on the Potomac River, where thousands of visitors crowded the resort during the summer months. Colonial Beach was platted in 1882 by Henry J. Kintz on the 650-acre White Point Farm. Alexander Graham Bell, inventor of the telephone, built two cottages there.* Courtesy of John C. Wilson and *The Westmoreland News*

Steamer Pier on the Potomac
Colonial Beach, Va.

Some of the 250 oyster boats gathered on the day in 1965 when the Virginia Commission of Fisheries opened, without public notice, some freshly-seeded public rock on Nomini Creek. In four days the oyster catch was harvested, with boats averaging 50 bushels each per day. In 1958 the regulation of oyster harvesting had begun following years of warfare among watermen who dredged illegally under cover of darkness or fog. Photograph by John Wilson, courtesy of the *Northumberland Echo.*

Richmond County

In December of 1656, "the inhabitants of the lower part of Lancaster County shewing their vast distance from the countie courts," the Grand Assembly (7th of the Commonwealth) ordered the division along the lines of the existing parishes, the lower county to retain the name of Lancaster, and the upper county to be named Rappahannock County. In 1692, Rappahannock County was further divided into Richmond and Essex counties. Since 1748 the county's business has been conducted at the courthouse in Warsaw.

Nowhere in the English colony of Virginia was there a better example than in Richmond County of the attempt to create a society like that found in England. Here, the owners of large estates assumed a role similar to that of the English aristocracy, with comparable social, economic and political power. Several outstanding homes of Virginia's ruling elite are still in existence in the county. Two of them, Sabine Hall and Mount Airy, are owned by descendants of the builders. In contrast, more than half of Richmond County's 18th century residents owned 200 acres or less. In 1790 the population was 6,985, and in 2000, was 8,809.

Constructed in 1748 under the direction of Landon Carter, the Richmond County Courthouse originally had an open gallery on each of two sides. The arcades were closed during an extensive renovation of the building by architect T. Buckler Chequiere in 1877. Formed in 1692 by division of old Rappahannock County, Richmond County celebrated its 300-year anniversary in 1992. Photograph by Thomas T. Waterman in 1938. Courtesy of the Library of Congress

The walls of the older portion of the Richmond County clerk's office, built in 1816 under the supervision of John Tayloe of Mount Airy, are made of blocks of stone two feet thick. In 1940, a visitor recorded that the interior was heated with an open fireplace and that there were "musty" records, recorded by professional scribes, who spelled "God" with a small "g" and "Rum" with a capital "R." (WPA, Virginia) The old clerk's office became a museum in 1992. Photograph in 1938 by Thomas T. Waterman. Courtesy of the Library of Congress

March Court in Warsaw was photographed in 1940. The building to the right houses the Northern Neck News, *founded in 1879.* Courtesy of John Wilson and Charles and Elizabeth Ryland

Sabine Hall, near Warsaw, was built by Landon Carter, one of the three sons of Robert "King" Carter, around 1735. Still owned by descendants of Landon Carter, the house is decorated with furniture and portraits that help to tell the family history. Included are some pieces from Corotoman, which burned in 1729, and the library of Landon Carter, whose classical reading was extensive. Photograph by C. O. Greene in 1940. Courtesy of the Library of Congress

First known as Tayloe's Quarter, the land on which Mount Airy stands was purchased by William Tayloe, the immigrant, in 1682. The present structure was completed in 1758 by John Tayloe II. Mount Airy is notable as an authentic Georgian mansion with ambitious use of stone. Although no architect has been identified, Virginia architect John Ariss has been suggested. The original interior, later destroyed by fire, was the work of William Buckland. Courtesy of the Library of Congress

Born in 1734, Francis Lightfoot Lee was the fifth child of Thomas Lee of Stratford Hall and his wife, Hannah Harrison Ludwell Lee. When in his mid-twenties, he moved to Loudoun County, settling on his portion of his father's 4500-acre tract. In 1769, Lee moved to Richmond County, from which he was elected to the House of Burgesses. He was elected to a seat in the first Continental Congress and was a signer of the Declaration of Independence. His home was Menokin, built by John Tayloe for his daughter Rebecca Tayloe, who married Lee in 1769. The house was in ruins when, in 1995, the Menokin Trust was organized for the purpose of restoration.
Courtesy of the Library of Virginia

Built in 1737 to replace an earlier structure, North Farnham Church included among its early parishioners the Tayloes of Mount Airy and the Carters of Sabine Hall. After disestablishment, the church was abandoned and used as a granary, a stable, a distillery, and a place for hogs, according to Bishop William Meade. It was damaged by bullets during the War of 1812, but was restored with the revival of the Episcopal Church in the 1830s. Stripped of its furnishings during the Civil War, and gutted by fire in 1887, it was again restored. The 18th century silver was returned in 1876. Photograph in 1934 by C. E. Peterson. Courtesy of the Library of Congress

Linden dates to the middle of the 18th century when the earliest portion of the house was built for members of the Dew family, who had owned the property since 1661. In 1977, Donald J. and Martha B. Orth purchased the house and painstakingly restored it to its early condition. This photograph shows the rear of the house with its long, sloping roof. Courtesy of Donald J. and Martha B. Orth

The monument to Congressman William Atkinson Jones, placed in St. John's churchyard in Warsaw, was presented as "A Tribute of gratitude of the Filipino People" in 1924 for a man who played a vital role in the movement to give independence to the Philippine Islands. St. John's Church was built in 1835. Photograph by Forest W. Patton. Courtesy of Richmond County Museum

King George County

In November of 1720, an act was passed by Virginia's General Assembly for the division of Richmond County, forming the new county of King George, named for the reigning king of England, George I. The first courthouse was built on land near Cleve, the seat of Charles Carter. Prior to the treaty of 1684, made by Lord Howard of Effingham, the land had been home to the Rappahannock Indians, who were pushed farther westward as the English settlers increased in number. The present courthouse was constructed in the village of King George in 1922, designed by the Fredericksburg architect, E. G. Heflin.

An early settler in King George County was William Fitzhugh, who moved into a part of the county that was then in Stafford County in the 1670s. Though he attained great wealth, Fitzhugh was concerned about the isolation of himself and his children. In 1686, he wrote Nicholas Hayward, "Society that is good & ingenious is very scarce, & seldom to be come at except in books. Good Education of children is almost impossible, & better to be never born than ill bred, but that which bears the greatest weight with me, for now I look upon my self to be in my declining age, is the want of spirituall help & comforts, of which this fertile Country in every thing, is barren and unfruitfull . . ." (*William Fitzhugh and His Chesapeake World*).

Few colonial homes remain in King George County, but the names of those early houses have sometimes been retained in subsequent structures. Important historic names which remain are Eagle's Nest, a Fitzhugh home; Cleve, the Carter home; Marmion, a Fitzhugh home; and Powhatan, built by Edward Thornton Tayloe and later home of the former ambassador to Ireland, Raymond R. Guest. There is also the site of Nanzattico, named for Indians who were there at the time of Captain John Smith.

Until the 20th century, the waterways in and near King George County provided a better means of travel than overland routes, resulting in the establishment of numerous ferries, among them Fitzhugh's ferry, which carried people, horses and supplies to and from Maryland. In the 19th century, steamboats began to replace ferries, greatly increasing opportunities for contact with other parts of the country.

In 1980, fifty-two percent of the population of King George County was employed by the federal government, and about a third of the residents worked outside the county. Many of those working for the federal government were employed by the Naval Surface Weapons Center at Dahlgren, where, in 1990, there were 3,899 employees.

From a population of 7,366 in 1790 the inhabitants had increased to only 16,803 in 2000 but growth was expected to occur rapidly as the Fredericksburg suburbs expanded.

George Louis, Elector of Hanover, was the great-grandson of King James I of England. George became King of England through the Act of Settlement upon the death of Queen Anne in 1714. George I spoke no English and chose to remain in Hanover while his ministers ruled England. Courtesy of the Library of Virginia

Born in 1651, William Fitzhugh came to Virginia in the early 1670s, settling on the Potomac River in what is now King George County. He became one of the leading figures in the area, practicing law with Giles Brent and serving in the Virginia House of Burgesses. When Fitzhugh died in 1701, he left 54,000 acres of land including a 21,966-acre tract in Fairfax County later known as Ravensworth. Among his descendants were the Fitzhughs of Marmion and Eagle's Nest in King George County, Chatham in Stafford County, and Ravensworth. Courtesy of the Virginia Historical Society

The courthouse of King George County was constructed in 1922. Formed from upper Richmond County in 1720, King George County's present boundaries were established in 1776, with some changes made in 1778. The village of King George is the county seat. On the courthouse grounds, a plain marble shaft was erected in honor of Confederate dead by the Ladies Memorial Association. Near the courthouse is the Lewis Egerton Smoot Memorial Library, given to King George County by Mrs. Smoot in honor of her husband. Courtesy of King George County

Constructed in the form of a Greek cross, St. Paul's Church resembles in plan Christ Church in Lancaster County, but it differs in the simplicity of its details. The church was built in 1766, though its Parish Register goes back to 1716 and an earlier building. The Scotsman, Rev. David Stuart, who was connected with the Royal House of Stuart, became rector of the parish in 1722. The 1721 communion service and the 1762 Bible survive. Photograph by Ralph E. Fall, courtesy of the Virginia Department of Historic Resources

Marmion was built around 1750 for the third William Fitzhugh and was sold to George Lewis, a nephew of George Washington, around 1785, remaining in the Lewis family until 1977. A paneled and painted drawing room from the house was removed for exhibition at the Metropolitan Museum of Art in New York. 1936 photo by Fred D. Nichols, courtesy of the Library of Congress

Born near Port Conway in King George County in 1751, James Madison grew up at Montpelier, his father's estate in Orange County. He was only 25 years old when elected to Virginia's first Constitutional Convention, and was a member of the Continental Congress, where his Virginia Plan served as an example to the writers of the Constitution of the United States. He served as president of the United States for two terms beginning in 1809, after having been Secretary of State for eight years under President Thomas Jefferson. Engraved by W. Wellstood from a portrait by Gilbert Stuart. Courtesy of the Library of Congress

Berry Plain circa 1800

Berry Plain, a venerable old frame house on a bend of the Rappahannock River, is named for the family who occupied it from the time of William Berry (1653-1721) until 1844. Then it was owned by John Fayette Dickinson, whose family lived on the place until 1959 and many of them are buried in the family graveyard near the house. Slave quarters and overseer's house add to the historic interest of the property. Courtesy of Joan and Tom Poland

Cleydael, built as a summer home for Dr. Richard H. Stuart, is of historical interest both because of the prominent King George family who lived there and for the visitors who sought refuge with the doctor and his family. In 1861, Annie and Agnes Lee, daughters of General Robert E. Lee, came to Cleydael (Clydale) after fleeing their home, Arlington House, in Alexandria County. The Lee girls were connected with the Stuart family through the marriage of their great-grandmother, Eleanor Calvert Custis, to Dr. David Stuart. John Wilkes Booth came seeking medical attention on April 23, 1865, after his attack on President Abraham Lincoln. Photo by Karen D. Steele. Courtesy of the Virginia Department of Historic Resources

Painted by artist John Shaw, the American bald eagle is seen rising from the Potomac near the Caledon Natural Area in King George County. In 1974, Mrs. Lewis Smoot donated 2500 acres of her Caledon estate to the state in her husband's memory. Caledon is on land acquired in the 17th century by John Alexander, the man for whom Alexandria was named. In 1985, the area was opened as a park. Courtesy of the artist, John Shaw

III

Fredericksburg

Captain John Smith mentioned the Rappahannock River in the journal he wrote as he journeyed from the Jamestown settlement to explore the Chesapeake Bay and its tributaries in 1608. A few years later, in 1613, sea Captain Samuel Argall wrote a letter to a friend in London describing the Falls of the Rappahannock River. He also wrote of the "kine" or buffaloes he saw grazing in the grasslands above the falls. The Indians who hunted there had long followed the practice of burning the naturally dense forests to create grasslands.

Realizing the potential for settlement in the area, the visionary and prosperous gentlewoman, Margaret Brent of Aquia applied for and received a colonial patent in 1655 for 1,000 acres on the south side of the Rappahannock one-quarter mile above the falls.

German explorer John Lederer mapped and explored the falls area and noted many of its natural resources in 1670. This stimulated interest among colonial land speculators including John Buckner, Robert Bryan and Thomas Royston, who received a grant of 2,000 acres in 1671 from Gov. William Berkeley. This tract on the south side of the Rappahannock below the falls was called the leaseland and frequently thereafter was so identified in the colonial records.

William Levingston leased a small parcel of the leaseland from Buckner and Royston when he and his wife Sukey moved to the wilderness in the early 1700s. They built thereon a house and kitchen. The Levingstons opened a coffee house about a mile below the falls on land which later became the center of Fredericksburg.

When more Europeans settled the area, a new county was formed by the colonial government from the earlier counties of Essex, King William and King and Queen, in 1720. It was named Spotsylvania after energetic and ambitious Alexander Spotswood, who served as Virginia's lieutenant governor from 1710 to 1722. The burgesses established the town of Fredericksburg by statute in 1728, on the Buckner and Royston leaseland in Spotsylvania County. In the same act, the town of Falmouth was established on William Todd's land on the north side of the river, above the falls. Some of the stated purposes mentioned that "peopling that remote part of the country will be encouraged, and trade and navigation may be increased." Public tobacco warehouses were established in both Falmouth and Fredericksburg in 1730 and a new ferry station between the two in 1732.

Because of the proximity of the river to the two towns and the fact that the main north-south road along the west side of the Chesapeake Bay crossed the western road from Williamsburg to Winchester in the Shenandoah Valley there, Fredericksburg and Falmouth were important colonial ports. In the second half of the 18th century, the combined trade of the two ports ranked twentieth among 43 ports and areas of North America in volume. During the American Revolution, Fredericksburg was of great importance to the colonists because of both materiel and men provided. Fielding Lewis' gunnery and Hunter's Iron Works furnished arms. Men associated with the town at one time or another served in the colonial forces, men including George Washington, Hugh Mercer, George Weedon, James Monroe, John Paul Jones and others.

Following the independence of the American colonies from Britain in 1783, there was not only a great westward movement of many Virginia residents but also major efforts to improve Virginia's transportation facilities. Turnpike roads, plank roads, canals, and later railroads were constructed.

The Civil War brought devastation to the town in the 1860s. Scars of the major battle in December 1862 may still be seen on some streets and buildings. During the war, the town changed hands seven times and local cemeteries were the final resting places for 17,000 soldiers who fell in battles there.

In the many decades between the early 1800s and the mid-1900s, steamboats and their commercial landings at Fredericksburg and other communities on the Potomac and Rappahannock rivers were the area's main links to the rest of the world. The Baltimore, Chesapeake & Atlantic Railway Company, the Maryland, Delaware and Virginia Railway Company and the Baltimore Steam Packet Company (The Old Bay Line) were the principal such trade and transportation companies.

As a municipality, Fredericksburg experienced significant changes over a number of years. It was incorporated as a city in 1879; in 1912, it adopted the country's first council-city manager form of government. The population had been 1,485 in 1790; it was 19,279 in 2000.

In order to protect old and historic buildings a non-profit preservation organization, Historic Fredericksburg Foundation, Inc., was chartered in 1955. In 1971 a 40-block area of downtown Fredericksburg, including relatively unchanged late 18th and early 19th century buildings, was placed on the National Register of Historic Places. More than 900 buildings considered worthy of preservation were included in the designated area.

The Visitor Center and Museum, at Lafayette Boulevard and Sunken Road, provides information and a self-guided tour of local Civil War battlefields in Fredericksburg, Chancellorsville, the Wilderness, Spotsylvania Court House and the "Stonewall" Jackson shrine.

Frederick Louis, Prince of Wales, was the person after whom Fredericksburg was named when it was established in 1728. He was born in Hanover in 1707, the eldest son of George II of England. He later married Augusta, daughter of Frederick II of Saxe-Gotha. The couple had seven children of whom the eldest became George III, following the death of his grandfather in 1760. A patron of music and painting, Frederick is shown playing the cello in this portrait by Philip Mercier. With him are his sisters, Anne, Princess Royal, Caroline and Amelia, for whom streets of Fredericksburg were named. Portrait courtesy of the National Portrait Gallery, London

The present Fredericksburg Courthouse was built on Princess Anne Street in 1852. It was designed in the Gothic style by James Renwick who was later the architect of the original building of the Smithsonian Institution complex and the Renwick Gallery in Washington, D. C.. In 1778 the county court function moved to the center of Spotsylvania County. Courtesy of the Virginia Department of Historic Resources

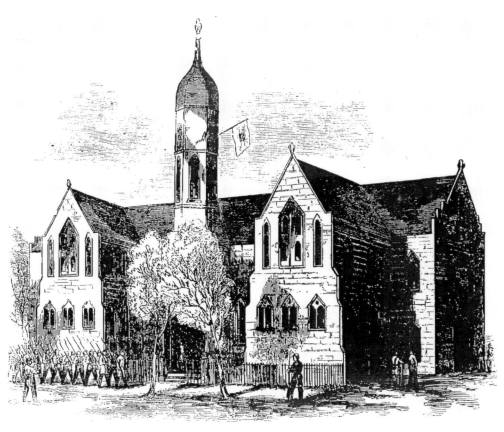

Kenmore was built by Fielding Lewis for his wife, Betty Washington Lewis, and their family. It was completed about 1756 and is an outstanding example of 18th century Tidewater Virginia design. Called "Millbrook" by the Lewises, the name "Kenmore" was given to the property by owner Sam Gordon in 1819.

During the Revolutionary War, Fielding Lewis and his friend, Charles Dick, operated a gunnery near Fredericksburg for the colonists and invested heavily with their own funds to aid in the cause of freedom from Great Britain. Photo by Flournoy, courtesy of the Virginia Chamber of Commerce

The ceiling of the Great Room in Kenmore is one of the finest examples of decorative plasterwork in America. After the work was completed in 1775, Fielding Lewis lent his "stucco man" to his brother-in-law, George Washington, to do the plasterwork ceiling decoration in the formal dining room at Mount Vernon. The house served as military headquarters and hospital during the Civil War, then was a boy's school. In 1922 it was purchased by the Kenmore Association which administers the property. Courtesy of the Virginia State Travel Service

The interior design of Federal Hill, constructed about 1755, was modeled after the exquisite work of architect William Buckland at statesman George Mason's Gunston Hall in Fairfax County. On Hanover Street, it was once the home of Robert Brooke, Virginia's governor from 1794-1796. Photo by Frances Benjamin Johnston, courtesy of the Library of Congress

This frame building on Caroline Street was constructed about 1760 and used as a residence by Charles Washington, youngest brother of George Washington, for twenty years. When Washington moved to the west and established the town now known as Charles Town, West Virginia, John Frazier leased the building and opened a tavern which he called the Golden Eagle. It was named the Rising Sun in 1821 by another owner and reverted to residential use in 1827. It is now a restored 18th century tavern. (Willis and Felder, *Fredericksburg*). Drawing courtesy of the artist, W. Scott Howson

Dr. Hugh Mercer was born in Aberdeen, Scotland in 1725 and graduated from the Aberdeen Medical School in 1744, coming to America two years later as a political refugee. He practiced medicine in Mercersburg, Pennsylvania until 1755. Wounded while serving in the Braddock expedition, he was with the Forbes expedition which captured Fort Duquesne in 1758. In 1776, he became first a colonel and then a brigadier general in the 3rd Virginia Line, and commander of the Flying Camp. He eventually fell at the Battle of Princeton, mortally wounded. He died on January 12, 1777. Pencil drawing by Colonel Trumbull, courtesy of the National Archives

Dr. Hugh Mercer settled in Fredericksburg after the French and Indian War and purchased, in 1771, a lot on the corner of Caroline and Amelia streets on which he established a doctor's office and apothecary shop. He bought Ferry Farm in Stafford County, across the river from Fredericksburg, from his friend and comrade in arms, George Washington. The apothecary shop museum presents information and exhibits about 18th and 19th century medicines and surgical procedures. It is owned by the Association for the Preservation of Virginia Antiquities. Photo by Frances Benjamin Johnston. Courtesy of the Library of Congress

George Washington purchased a house on Charles Street in Fredericksburg in 1772 for his mother, Mary, so she could live near her daughter Betty Washington Lewis and her family, and her son Charles. An addition was built on the house, where she lived until her death in 1789. The structure was acquired in 1890 by the Association for the Preservation of Virginia Antiquities, and has been restored and furnished with period pieces. The Garden Club of Virginia restored the garden in 1968. Courtesy of Virginia Department of Historic Resources

Born in Westmoreland County in 1758, James Monroe was president of the United States from 1816 until 1824. Prior to that he was an envoy to France, Secretary of War and Secretary of State. His long career of service to his country also included that of Revolutionary War soldier, member of the Virginia Constitutional Convention, delegate to the General Assembly of Virginia, and member of the Senate of the United States. He assisted with negotiations for the Louisiana Purchase and served as the American minister in Spain. As president, Monroe enunciated the doctrine which bears his name. His law office in Fredericksburg has become a museum. Courtesy of the Library of Congress

Matthew Fontaine Maury (1806-1873) was born near Fredericksburg. He married Ann Hull Herndon of Fredericksburg in 1834 and the couple had eight children. Maury's published scholarly writings about navigation, winds and ocean currents brought him international fame and recognition from mariners, scientists and commercial entrepreneurs. He was appointed the first superintendent of the Naval Observatory in Washington, D. C., and earned the nickname "Pathfinder of the Seas." Bronze bust of Maury by Edward Virginius Valentine. Courtesy of the National Portrait Gallery, Smithsonian Institution

On a site on Sophia Street at William Street beside the Rappahannock River and Chatham Bridge, this stone warehouse was built at the beginning of the War of 1812, a successor to several structures lost to floods and a fire. It was probably used initially to store arms and ammunition, and during the Civil War was hit five times and used as a morgue for casualties. After the war it served as a brewery, a feed and fertilizer warehouse, and a fish-curing factory. Administered by the Historic Fredericksburg Foundation, the building was leased to the Fredericksburg chapter of the Archeological Society of Virginia. Photo in the 1920s by Frances Benjamin Johnston, courtesy of the Library of Congress

In 1814, Fredericksburg's city council ordered that a new city hall and market house be built on Princess Anne Street to replace the building which had been erected for the purpose about 1765. It was in this new building that a reception was held for Lafayette during his tour of the United States in 1824 and 1825. It was used for city offices until 1982. The city hall and its adjacent market square are now occupied by the Fredericksburg Area Museum and Cultural Center. Photo in the 1920s by Frances Benjamin Johnston, courtesy of the Library of Congress

The auction block at the corner of William and Charles streets is a memento of antebellum days. The plaque states: "Auction Block. Fredericksburg's Principal Auction Site in Pre-Civil War Days for Slaves and Property. 1984, HFFT." The original building on the same corner was a tavern but was replaced by a brick building in 1843. Still standing, it has been called by various names including the U. S. Hotel, the Planters Hotel, the R. T. Knox and Sons office, and the Knoxanna Building. Courtesy of the photographer, Richard Netherton

Brompton, the official residence of the president of Mary Washington College at Sunken Road and Hanover Street, was bought in 1824 by John Lawrence Marye, son and grandson of St. George's Parish Episcopal ministers. Damaged during the Civil War, it was repaired and altered after hostilities ceased. The former women's college, coeducational since 1970, operates a unique Center for Historic Preservation which, in addition to supporting the undergraduate program in preservation, provides specialized services to preservation organizations and interested individuals throughout Virginia. Photo by Frances Benjamin Johnston, courtesy of the Library of Congress

This early 1900s photo taken near Fredericksburg shows some of the problems associated with farming, travel and commerce. Before the hard-surfacing of thoroughfares, each year in Virginia dirt roads became large mud bogs due to freezing and thawing or heavy rains. Courtesy of the Virginia Department of Transportation

The Richmond, Fredericksburg & Potomac Railroad built a graceful arched bridge over the Rappahannock at Fredericksburg in 1927. Shown here is passenger train No. 21, "The Silver Star," crossing the bridge behind Engine No. 621, the "Governor Richard Henry Lee." A number of locomotives on the RF&P were named after prominent Virginians. The railroad became CSX in 1992. Courtesy of the RF&P Railroad

IV

Stafford County

Formed in 1664 from the western part of Westmoreland County, Stafford originally included what are now Prince William, Fairfax, Fauquier, Loudoun, Arlington, and part of King George counties. On his 1608 map, Captain John Smith accurately located streams and Indian villages, including Patowmack, the future location of the town of Marlborough, where Pocahontas, daughter of the powerful Indian leader, Powhatan, was captured in 1612 by Captain Argall and taken to Jamestown.

Among the early settlers in the region that became Stafford County was Giles Brent, a Catholic who crossed the Potomac River from Maryland in 1647 to settle on the north side of Aquia Creek. A kinsman of Lord Baltimore, Brent had married Kittamaquad, daughter of the ruler of the Piscataway Indians. His sisters, Margaret and Mary, joined him at the Aquia settlement. When King James II, a Catholic, ascended the English throne in 1685, Parson John Waugh, of Overwharton Parish in Stafford County, led his followers to believe that a Catholic invasion from Maryland was imminent, resulting in "Parson Waugh's Tumult."

Stafford County was first in Potomac Parish, established around 1654, and divided into Overwharton and Chotank (now St. Paul's) before 1680. The churches of Overwharton Parish were Potomac, Aquia, and Cedar in Falmouth. St. Paul's Parish was in the portion of Stafford that became part of King George County.

Soon after Stafford County was established, a courthouse was built south of Potomac Creek; another was built on the site of the new town of Marlborough in 1692. When that courthouse was destroyed by fire around 1718, the court was moved to Stoneman's Landing, where it met until moved to its present site in 1783. The existing courthouse was constructed in 1916.

The early economy of Stafford County was based on tobacco, which was used for exchange in the colony.

As the tobacco trade prospered, slaves were brought in to work on the large plantations, and ports were established along the rivers for the exchange of goods. As the price of tobacco fell near the end of the 17th century, other crops grew in importance. Grains were exported in large quantities, and flour mills, iron foundries, and fishing industries dotted the landscape. The port of Falmouth, established in 1728, had numerous warehouses through which goods from the interior of Virginia were loaded on ships bound for the Atlantic via the Rappahannock River and the Chesapeake Bay. There were, however, always risks, as reported in 1771, when nine hundred hogsheads of tobacco were floated out of warehouses in Falmouth in a freshet or sudden flood.

In the 19th century, major steamboat landings were built on the Potomac River at Potomac and Aquia creeks. Boat passengers going south continued on from here in stagecoaches. The Richmond, Fredericksburg, and Potomac railroad was incorporated in 1834 and the track to Aquia Creek from Richmond opened in 1842. The railroad also acquired a half interest in the Washington and Fredericksburg Steamboat Company and travel between Washington and Richmond was a combination of both means until after the Civil War.

In the 20th century, the automobile became the preferred means of personal travel and better roads were demanded. In 1923 a state highway system was established and improved road building was begun on a pay-as-you-go basis. Soon Stafford County found itself in an advantageous situation halfway between Washington and Richmond along US Route 1.

In 1790 there were a total of 9,588 persons counted in Stafford County. The county's population increased slowly until the end of the 20th century, and the population was 92,446 in 2000. From a rural, agricultural region, Stafford County was fast becoming part of the Washington and Fredericksburg suburban area.

Formed from Westmoreland County in 1664, Stafford County was named for the English shire of the same name. The courthouse shown is believed to have been constructed c. 1840 on the site of a building erected in 1783 on land given for the purpose by William Fitzhugh of Chatham. Nearby were a clerk's office and a jail. This courthouse was demolished in 1916 and replaced by another building at the same location. Many of Stafford County's records were lost during the Civil War. From the postcard collection of Tony Chaves

Unveiled in 1930 by the Catholic Woman's Club of Richmond, the crucifix on U.S. Route 1 in Stafford County memorializes the English-speaking Catholic settlement of the 17ᵗʰ century. The crucifix is 30 feet high and was cast by Georg J. Lober. The plaque on the crucifix states that Giles Brent petitioned for and obtained a proclamation of religious tolerance from James II of England. Nearby is the Brent family cemetery, recently an archeological study site. Courtesy of the photographer Richard Netherton

Located at Widewater in Stafford County, Richland's history goes back to the 17th century settlement begun by Giles Brent at Aquia. The house is on land acquired by Brent in the 1650s, soon after his coming to Virginia. A c.1725 house was burned by the British during the American Revolution, but was rebuilt by 1787, when it was the home of Daniel Carroll Brent and his wife, Anne Fenton Lee. In 1821 the house, with 1,906 acres of land, was sold to William Henry Fitzhugh of Chatham and Ravensworth. After the Civil War, it became the home of General Fitzhugh Lee, later governor of Virginia. Photograph by Calder Loth, courtesy of the Virginia Department of Historic Resources

Aquia Church in Overwharton Parish, was built within older brick walls in 1757 to replace an earlier church which was partially damaged by fire. William Copein was the mason and Mourning Richards the contractor. The exterior design is unusually sophisticated for the rural setting and the triple-tiered pulpit is striking in the austere interior. Overwharton Parish was served by John Moncure, who become minister in 1738. Of Scottish descent, he established a family which has remained prominent in the county ever since. Photograph by Edward Breitenbach, courtesy of the Fairfax County Public Library

Born in 1805, Judge Richard Cassius Lee Moncure became Commonwealth's Attorney for Stafford County in 1826 and later served a number of terms in the Virginia House of Delegates. He served in the Constitutional Convention of 1850-51, representing Alexandria, Fairfax, Prince William and Stafford Counties. Following the adoption of the new constitution, Moncure was elected to the Court of Appeals. Judge Moncure lived at Glencairne. Painted by R. McGill Machall, Judge Moncure's portrait hangs in the Stafford County Courthouse. Courtesy of Thomas M. Moncure, Jr., Clerk of the Court

Near Passapatanzy in Stafford County is the White Oak Primitive Baptist Church and its cemetery. The simplicity of the structure reflects the precept of the denomination, that individuals should derive their instruction directly from the Bible and not through the interpretation of others. It is believed to have been built in the 1780s on land given to the congregation by John Moncure. Courtesy of the Virginia Department of Historic Resources

Ferry Farm, which lies across the Rappahannock River from Fredericksburg, became the home of young George Washington in 1738 when Augustine Washington moved his family there to be near his iron furnace on Accokeek Creek. The only building remaining on Ferry Farm from George Washington's day is the small shed where he is believed to have learned surveying. Photographed by Frances Benjamin Johnston, courtesy of the Library of Congress

Hunter's Iron Works was established by James Hunter on land purchased around 1750 from the owners of Accokeek Furnace, which had been built by George Washington's father and some partners in England for the production of pig iron. During the American Revolution, it was an important supplier of war materiel and was given special protection by order of Thomas Jefferson, then governor of Virginia. On the property in 1798 were a forge 128x40 feet, a merchant mill, a grist mill, a sawmill, a nailery, a tanyard, workers' shops, and houses for managers and workmen. Courtesy of the Virginia Department of Historic Resources

Among the warehouses remaining in Falmouth is one which belonged to Basil Gordon, a Scotsman who came to America with his brother Samuel and settled in Falmouth, a major port on the Rappahannock River, established in 1728. Another old warehouse in Falmouth was owned by Duff Green, a leading citizen and financier. He had a cotton mill in a large brick building on the main thoroughfare of the town. Basil Gordon's warehouse is in the Falmouth Historic District. Photograph by Frances Benjamin Johnston, courtesy of the Library of Congress

The Temperance Tavern in historic Falmouth was originally a warehouse built in 1820, and converted into a tavern for sailors, travelers and others who might require its services. It was built by William Brooke, Jr. and housed goods traded in the early nineteenth century. Around 1835 Brooke turned the structure into an inn and dwelling. The Temperance Tavern is in the Falmouth Historic District. Photograph by Frances Benjamin Johnston, courtesy of the Library of Congress

Painted in watercolor by Benjamin Henry Latrobe in 1806, "View on the Potomac River" shows two large boulders that stood near Aquia at Clifton in Stafford County. Aquia's freestone was the basic material used for the construction of the United States Capitol and the White House in the City of Washington. It was used in the construction of numerous historic houses and churches in Northern Virginia. Courtesy of the Maryland Historical Society

Chatham was built by William Fitzhugh, a descendant of the 17th century immigrant of that name. Completed c. 1771, the house was made of local brick and timber, and was named for William Pitt, Earl of Chatham. Among Fitzhugh's friends was George Washington. With the coming of the Civil War, the property was occupied by General Irvin McDowell, who entertained President Lincoln there. It also was a hospital where both Clara Barton and Walt Whitman worked. Its last owner was John Lee Pratt, who was born on a King George County farm and rose to be one of the wealthiest men in America. After his death in 1975, the property became part of the National Park Service. Photo Francis Benjamin Johnston, courtesy of the Library of Congress.

Judge Richard Henry Lee Chichester was born in Fairfax County in 1870, but spent most of his life in Stafford County. He held every judicial position in the Commonwealth, culminating in his appointment to the Supreme Court of Appeals in 1925. He lived at Glencairne, which has been the home of six generations of Moncures and Chichesters. Commonwealth's Attorney Daniel Chichester, the latest owner, is a skilled carpenter, who has furnished the home with his own copies of museum furniture. Courtesy of Thomas M. Moncure, Jr., Clerk of the Court

Katherine Harwood Waller spent her childhood at Clifton, which stands on land acquired by William Waller and George Master around 1627. She married Robert Smith Barrett, a rector of Aquia Church. Kate's concern for prostitutes and unwed mothers led her to study medicine in order to better care for her charges. She became president and general superintendent of the Florence Crittenden Home and was active in many other charitable organizations. Courtesy of the Library of Congress

Belmont was constructed in 1761 by John Dixon. In 1916 the estate was purchased by the artist Gari Melchers. The winner of numerous medals in exhibitions in the United States and Europe, Melchers was commissioned to paint allegories on peace and war for the Library of Congress. His wife, Corrine, who was also an artist, bequeathed Belmont to the State of Virginia. The estate is administered by Mary Washington College, Fredericksburg, Virginia. Courtesy of Belmont, The Gari Melchers Memorial Gallery

V

Prince William County

Prince William County was established in 1731 and was named after William Augustus, Duke of Cumberland, son of King George II of England. The first of the county's six court buildings was soon erected on the south side of the Occoquan River near the Potomac on the "Woodbridge" plantation of George Mason II.

Also in 1731, the "Brent Town Tract" of 30,000 acres, originally meant for establishment of a colony of Huguenots, proved unsuccessful. The land was equally divided between the four original partners, Nicholas Hayward, Robert Bristow, Robert Brent, and Richard Foote.

Henry Lee II and his bride, Lucy Grymes moved to the family property in Prince William they called "Leesylvania." It was later the birthplace of Gen. Henry Lee III, ("Light Horse Harry"), Governor of Virginia, and father of General Robert E. Lee; Attorney General Charles Lee; Representative Richard Bland Lee; and Edmund Jennings Lee, Mayor of Alexandria. Leesylvania is now a Virginia State Park.

The building of the Orange and Alexandria Rail Road, begun in 1848, was heralded as a great advance in commerce and communication. The line was completed to Tudor Hall (later named Manassas) in 1860 just as the Civil War conflict was developing. The principal reason for the growth of Manassas was the junction of the Orange & Alexandria and Manassas Gap railroads at that point.

In the late 19th century, the growth of public schools increased opportunities for white youth under the new Underwood Virginia Constitution. Manassas resident Jennie Dean realized that such opportunities were not as fully available to her African-American community. By dint of her great energy and persuasive powers, she was able to persuade prominent business people and philanthropists to join her in sponsoring the Manassas Industrial School for Colored Youth. This regional educational institution provided opportunities for youth of Prince William County and neighboring areas well into the 20th century.

The Quantico Marine Base was built during World War I and several other Federal government reservations lie within the county's boundaries. Thousands of acres of public parklands have been dedicated in Prince William County. The 400-acre Conway Robinson Memorial State Forest was established in 1938, and in 1940, 1,604 acres of land on which the First and Second Battles of Manassas were fought in 1861 and 1862 received a new designation, "Manassas National Battlefield Park." In the 1990s, more acreage was added to the park through a controversial "legislative taking." In 1998, Prince William Forest Park included 18,572 acres.

In an effort to revitalize the downtown area, develop tourism, and encourage historic preservation, 207 buildings, mostly in Old Town Manassas, were placed on the National Register of Historic Places in July 1988. In addition, the Manassas Museum was expanded to include several local historic sites and buildings.

A large commercial mall, Potomac Mills, was built in a pasture beside I-95 in the county in 1985. With about 170 discount and outlet stores, by 1994 the complex was not only a shopping destination but also the top tourist attraction in Virginia, with 10 million visitors a year. In the 1990s, the Walt Disney Company sought to take advantage of local growth and regional tourism, acquiring by purchase or options 3,000 acres of land near Haymarket. Their plan to develop a new theme park to be called "Disney's America" proved to be an unpopular one with local residents and historians. The Disney plan failed.

In 1790, Prince William county's population was 11,615; in the 2000 census, the number was 280,813.

Prince William County was formed from parts of Stafford and King George counties in 1731, and named for William Augustus, Duke of Cumberland and son of King George II. As head of the British army in the reign of George II, Cumberland became interested in American affairs as a means of countering French influence worldwide. In 1755, when Virginia's governor Dinwiddie asked for help in dealing with French and Indian encroachments in western lands claimed by Virginia, Cumberland sent troops, led by General Edward Braddock, to march from Alexandria against the French in western Pennsylvania. The campaign ended in disaster for the British and Virginians, but it began a war which eventually brought Canada and the mid-west under British control. Portrait courtesy of The Manassas Museum

Shown in this postcard view is the fifth courthouse to serve Prince William County. Built of local sandstone and brick, it was in use from 1894 to 1984 and still stands on the corner of Lee and Grant avenues. It was the scene of the Manassas National Jubilee of Peace in 1911, when President William Howard Taft was the honored speaker. The sixth courthouse was built in 1984 as the Judicial Center at the west end of Lee Avenue. From the postcard collection of Tony Chaves

Rippon Lodge was built by Richard Blackburn about 1730. Sketches of the house and the Potomac River view from it were made in 1796 by Benjamin Latrobe, architect of the Capitol in Washington. Photo by John O. Bistrup courtesy of the Library of Congress

The brick farmhouse called Bel Air, located near Minnieville, was built about 1740 by the Ewell family. The Rev. Mason Locke Weems, early biographer of George Washington, married one of the Ewell daughters and made Bel Air his home from 1809 until his death in 1825. He is buried in the family cemetery. Drawing courtesy of the Virginia Department of Historic Resources

Mason Locke "Parson" Weems' biography of George Washington was published in numerous editions and successfully peddled by Weems up and down the East Coast for the Matthew Cary Publishing Company of Philadelphia. He invented the well-loved story of the cherry tree. The house in which he lived in Dumfries from 1798 to 1802 is now the Weems-Botts Museum. Weems portrait from Dyckinck, *Encyclopedia of American Literature*, 1856

The flour and grist mill and John Ballendine's home, Rockledge, shown here, were constructed in 1759. The miller's house is now the home of Historic Occoquan, and the 19th century iron truss bridge was dislodged during Hurricane Agnes in June 1972 and washed downstream. It was replaced by a modern concrete highway bridge built downstream across the Occoquan River. The shadowy ruin to the right of the bridge on this postcard, postmarked in 1912, was once a large cotton mill built by Nathaniel Janney in 1828. It ran 1,000 spindles until the mill was burned during the Civil War.
From the postcard collection of Tony Chaves

The Beverly Mill on Broad Run in Thoroughfare Gap was an impressive stone structure representing Virginia's important early milling industry. On the boundary line between Prince William and Fauquier counties, beside modern U. S. Interstate Route 66, the first three stories were built before 1759 and were operated by John Chapman. The top two stories were added in the 1850s. It is a local tradition that the mill supplied meal to troops of five wars and was a scene of fighting during the Second Manassas Campaign, August 1862. The mill was grinding approximately 100,000 bushels of grain annually until the 1940s. The mill, now in ruins, burned in 1998. Photograph courtesy of the Library of Virginia

William Grayson (c. 1742-1790), a son of a successful merchant, was born in Prince William County. Educated in England, he practiced law in Dumfries. An early advocate of American rights, he signed the Leedstown Resolutions of 1766 opposing the Stamp Act. He rose to the rank of colonel, commanded a regiment and was appointed one of George Washington's aides-de-camp. Appointed to Virginia's House of Delegates in 1784, he later went to the Continental Congress. He was chosen to be one of Virginia's first two senators in the Federal government under the new Constitution. Portrait courtesy of the Library of Virginia

St. Paul's Episcopal Church was originally built at Haymarket in 1801 and was used as a district courthouse for Fairfax, Fauquier, Loudoun and Prince William counties until 1807. It was later used as an academy and then by several church denominations. First used as an Episcopal church in 1822 it was consecrated by Bishop William Meade in 1834. The building was burned during the Civil War but was rebuilt in 1867. Photograph courtesy of the Arlington County Public Library

The Brentsville courthouse was built in the 1820s and was Prince William County's fourth of six courthouses. It is now the oldest public building in the county. While occupied by Union troops during the Civil War, many public records there were destroyed or stolen by the soldiers. It remained the county courthouse until by referendum Manassas became the county seat in 1892 and a new courthouse was completed two years later. Photograph by Birchfield, courtesy of the Arlington County Public Library

Liberia was built about 1825 by William J. Weir on part of Robert "King" Carter's Lower Bull Run Tract. During the Civil War, the house was a headquarters for Union General Irvin McDowell. President Abraham Lincoln and Secretary of War Edwin Stanton visited McDowell at Liberia on June 19, 1862, after the general was injured when he fell off his horse. At another time, President Jefferson Davis visited Liberia when Confederate General Beauregard had his headquarters there. It is said that "King" Carter divided a tract of land into twelve parcels which he designated by the signs of the zodiac. Subsequently, "Liberia" became a corruption of its original name, "Libra." Photograph courtesy of the Library of Virginia

A Union Army Signal Corps veteran and a lawyer from New York, George Carr Round settled in Manassas in 1868, after deciding to seek his fortune in Virginia. An advocate of education, he was appointed the Town's first Superintendent of Public Schools. He also served as a member of the Virginia General Assembly, as a charter member of the Manassas Town Council, and as the Town Clerk.. In 1911, he served as the chairman of the Peace Jubilee held to commemorate the 50th anniversary of the Battle of First Manassas. Courtesy of The Manassas Museum System

Annaburg was a summer home built by Robert Portner, a Prussian by birth, in the early 1890s. He emigrated to the United States in 1853, eventually making his fortune as a brewer in Alexandria. The mansion is set on twenty acres of landscaped grounds and gardens which at one time included the historic house, Liberia. The building has since 1964 been used as a nursing home and is now part of the Prince William Hospital Health Care Center. Photograph courtesy of The Manassas Museum System

Jennie Dean was born c. 1852 in Prince William County of slave parents belonging to the Cushing and Newman families. As an adult she worked as a domestic in Washington and became dedicated to the task of providing education for black students in Virginia. Founder of the Manassas Industrial School for Colored Youth in 1893, she was able to raise funds to buy land and to acquire needed materials from philanthropists who were interested in her cause, among whom was Andrew Carnegie. Miss Dean was chosen "Woman of the Century, Deceased" during the Centennial celebration of Manassas in 1973. Photograph courtesy of The Manassas Museum System

The Manassas Town Band, shown here in the early 1900s, gave local citizens an opportunity to play brass instruments and provide community entertainment. Manassas also had an orchestra, theater productions and dances in Nichol's Hall, and residents and visitors were entertained by traveling circuses, shows and plays. Eastern College provided many educational and cultural opportunities as part of their regular program. Photograph courtesy of The Manassas Museum System

The first Prince William Hotel was built by Robert Portner in 1904 but it burned in 1910. It stood between Grant Avenue and West Street on the south side of the railroad. The second or "New" Prince William Hotel was built on the corner of Main and Center streets in 1912. Later called the Stonewall Jackson Hotel, it was demolished in the 1960s and the Olde Town Inn was erected on the site, serving an automobile-driving public. From the postcard collection of Tony Chaves

The Dixie Moving Picture Theatre was located on the west side of Main Street between Center Street and the railroad tracks. It was typical of a number of grand structures for film entertainment which were built all around Northern Virginia in the first quarter of the 20th century. This view was taken about 1915. From the postcard collection of Tony Chaves

This photograph of the Richmond-Washington highway (U.S. Route 1) at Dumfries in 1919 illustrates the condition of unpaved roads of the time, reported to be "six feet wide and nine feet deep," in the words of former Virginia State Road Commissioner Brig. Gen. James A. Anderson. Behind the mired automobile is the hostelry known variously since its construction in the late 1700s as Williams' Ordinary, Love's Tavern, the Stagecoach Inn and the Old Hotel. Courtesy of the Virginia Department of Transportation

The same section of U.S. Route 1 is shown in this 1933 photograph taken after an all-weather concrete roadway had been built by the Virginia Department of Highways. Courtesy of the Virginia Department of Transportation

The Piedmont Dairy Festival was patterned after Winchester's successful Apple Blossom Festival. It was held on the grounds of the Portners' Annaburg estate in Manassas beginning in 1931, as a Northern Virginia regional effort to promote an increased use of local dairy products. An elaborate pageant (shown here) was presented in 1935. The event was discontinued in 1937. Photograph courtesy of The Manassas Museum System

The Manassas Museum interprets the history of the Northern Piedmont region, the Battles of First and Second Manassas, and the post-Civil War development of Manassas. Founded in 1973, the Museum is currently located in a 6,000 square foot structure designed by architect Carlton Abbott, of Williamsburg, Virginia. The Manassas Museum operates six additional properties including the Manassas Industrial School and Jennie Dean Memorial Site; the Mayfield and Cannon Branch Civil War Earthwork Fortifications; the Historic Southern Railway Depot; the 1907 Hopkins Candy Factory, and Liberia, an 1825 plantation house. Courtesy of The Manassas Museum System

The Manassas Industrial School for Colored Youth was founded by Jennie Dean in 1893 and opened the following year. It was modeled on Tuskegee Institute and benefitted from the interest of Booker T. Washington in early years. Students came from all over Virginia, at least ten other states and the District of Columbia. In 1938 it became a public regional high school for African-American students, funded and operated by Fairfax, Fauquier and Prince William counties. In 1995, the Manassas Museum dedicated a memorial to Miss Jennie Dean at the site where the school once stood. From the postcard collection of Tony Chaves

VI

Fairfax County

Standing on the border of North and South, beside the historic Potomac route to the west, Fairfax County has for over three hundred years been a meeting place for the personalities and events which shaped the life of the nation. Although its best-known former resident is George Washington, whose restored home, Mount Vernon, is seen by more than a million visitors each year, a host of others, great and small, have in their own ways contributed to this shaping process. Fairfax County today is the hub of Northern Virginia, and one of the fastest growing regions in the state.

Four attempts had been made to divide Prince William County (in 1732, 1736, 1738, and 1740) and were denied by the Assembly, until William Fairfax, cousin of Thomas, Sixth Lord Fairfax, was elected a burgess from Prince William County, as was Thomas Harrison. The two men were successful in having the Virginia Assembly pass a bill on June 19, 1742, establishing the new county named Fairfax, effective December 1, 1742. The location of the county courthouse has been in three different places: Tysons Corner, 1742 - 1752; Alexandria, 1752 - 1800; and in Fairfax from 1800 to the present time.

About 1735, while his property was included within the boundaries of Prince William County, Captain Augustine Washington moved his family, including his infant son George, from Wakefield to the Little Hunting Creek Plantation, later renamed Mount Vernon. In 1739 the family moved back to Ferry Farm on the Rappahannock across from Fredericksburg, in Stafford County. George, when he became a teenager, moved to Mount Vernon to live with his older half brother, Lawrence, and his family in 1748. When Lawrence died four years later, George inherited Mount Vernon and bought out her life interest in the estate from his sister-in-law, Ann Fairfax Washington. In 1759, George married Martha Dandridge Custis, a wealthy young widow with two children, John and Patsy. Patsy died in her teens. John married Eleanor Calvert and the couple had four surviving children. John "Jackie" Custis died after the battle of Yorktown in 1781 and their two younger children, G. W. P. Custis and Eleanor, grew up at Mount Vernon. Later, Custis became master of Arlington House and "Nelly" became mistress of Woodlawn, near Belvoir, the old Fairfax estate.

After the Revolutionary War, in which statesman George Mason and General George Washington of Fairfax County played key roles, there was an exodus of local population as residents moved west to obtain new land and new lives. In 1790, the county's population was 12,320. By the 1830s, towns had begun to be established inland from the Potomac River. Fairfax County's seat of government was officially changed to the crossroads of the Little River Turnpike and the old Ox Road. Here the third courthouse was built and opened for business in 1800, and locally called by the name of the postal designation, Fairfax Court House, rather than the name "Providence" designated in the Virginia General Assembly statute. For the next 200 years, events, sometimes of national significance, brought major changes in the land and its people.

The Civil War, 1861-1865, caused major devastation from which recovery was slow. The coming of the automobile, the vast expansion of the Federal government's bureaucracy during and after World Wars I and II, and the influx of population provided workers for all levels of government, technology, goods and services, and public and private schools. In 1929, the Industrial Directory of Virginia reported that the dairy industry, poultry raising and market gardening and the raising of cattle, sheep and hogs were principal interests of Fairfax farmers. Industrial operations in the county were represented in paper, pulp wood cutting and flour and feed mills. In the 2000 census, the population was 969,749.

The rural aspect of the county has almost disappeared now. Computers, sophisticated communications, and other modern developments have urbanized most of the county. Education and training of skilled professionals to supply the needs of the work force are major concerns at all levels.

Lives of the general population through time are not forgotten in the county's preservation effort. The old courthouse, stately homes, churches, schools, country stores, water mills, a drovers' roadside inn, railroad stations, a jet-age airport, period gardens, farm houses and 18th, 19th, and 20th century demonstration farms all provide educational experiences and enlightenment for both county residents and visitors. Numerous living history groups, archaeologists, special programs, and reenactors stimulate remembrances of people, events and objects from both the recent and distant past.

James Wren, an early architect in Fairfax County, designed the courthouse completed at the crossroads of the Ox Road and Little River Turnpike in 1800, the third for the county. The building reflected an architectural style that originated in the arcaded two-story market halls of Flanders and the Netherlands. Wren's design for the Fairfax Courthouse was copied by several other Virginia counties that built courthouses in the first quarter of the nineteeth century. Courtesy of the artist, Gloria Matthews

Authorities in both the United States and Great Britain consider this to be the oldest and most complete set of English standards extant in the world. Made in London, these weights and measures, engraved "County of Fairfax, 1744," were used for more than 100 years at the Port of Alexandria. They are now on display in the museum of the George Washington Masonic Memorial. Courtesy of the Alexandria-Washington Lodge No. 22, A.F. & A.M., Alexandria, Virginia

The building of the Mount Vernon mansion was gradual, beginning with Lawrence Washington's modest little cottage. His brother George made many alterations after he acquired the residence. The most striking feature of the mansion is the two-story square-columned piazza on the river front. Courtesy of the Virginia Department of Conservation and Economic Development

George Washington was born in 1732 at Wakefield in Westmoreland County and at age 16 moved to Mount Vernon to live with his brother Lawrence. In addition to early military service in Virginia, George Washington served Fairfax County as a burgess, a justice and church vestryman. He served his country as general of the Revolutionary armies and as its first president under the federal Constitution. He was proud of being a farmer at Mount Vernon. Print by Currier in the 1850s

Gunston Hall was built by George Mason IV, in 1758. It is located on the Potomac River. William Buckland was Mason's indentured servant and a talented designer who incorporated many new ideas into the mansion's architecture. After his indenture, Buckland did admirable work for a number of other Virginia homeowners. Courtesy of Gunston Hall

George Mason of Gunston Hall was typical of Tidewater Virginia's gentlemen-planters at the height of the tobacco trade. He owned and managed extensive lands and numerous slaves. He took an active part in public affairs, serving at various times on the parish vestry, the county court, and in the House of Burgesses. In 1774, he drafted the Fairfax Resolves, and in 1776 wrote the Virginia Constitution and Virginia Declaration of Rights on which the Federal Bill of Rights was based. Painting by Dominic Boudet, c. 1811, after John Hesselius, c. 1750. Courtesy of Gunston Hall

The Falls Church was built of brick in 1769 to a design by architect James Wren to replace a wooden church built in the same spot in 1734. It is of a simple design, like many Anglican churches of the 18th century. It was used for military purposes during both the Revolutionary and Civil Wars. The postal village, town and eventually city were named after the church. The building still serves an active congregation. Courtesy of the Library of Congress

The parish church performed many of the social services in the community and along with the local county court was the training ground for self-government in colonial Virginia. Serving as a court justice or an Anglican church vestryman demanded a high order of leadership in local affairs. The rosters of vestrymen in the 18th century in Virginia carried the names of many leaders in the long journey to independence and nationhood. Shown here is Pohick Church of Truro Parish, on whose vestry served the families of Washington, Fairfax and Mason. Courtesy of Mount Vernon Ladies' Association of the Union

Sully Plantation was owned by Richard Bland Lee, first member of the House of Representatives from Northern Virginia. He proposed that Congress establish the Federal City of Washington at its present location. He supervised the construction of the house at Sully in 1794. The museum house and grounds, administered by the Fairfax County Park Authority, are across Route 28 from Dulles International Airport. Sketch courtesy of the artist, Gloria Matthews

The Ravensworth grant was the largest ever to be made in Fairfax County. The 22,000-acre tract was acquired by the Fitzhugh family in 1694. A large mansion house was built about 1800 by William Fitzhugh of Chatham. The house was burned in 1926. The handsome brick stable and carriage house was razed for a housing development in the 1960s.

An historical marker was placed at the Ravensworth site on Port Royal Road near Braddock Road and the Capital Beltway on September 11, 1993.
Courtesy of the Library of Congress

The Georgian-style Woodlawn mansion was designed for Lawrence and Eleanor Custis Lewis by William Thornton, first architect of the U. S. Capitol. It was built about 1805 on land given to the couple by Lewis' uncle, George Washington. In the 1950s, the house was purchased by a group of preservationists and given to the National Trust for Historic Preservation. It was the first National Trust property to be opened to the public. Drawing courtesy of the artist, Judith B. Pixton

In colonial times and the early 1800s, the water-powered grist mill represented the high point of mechanical development and engineering skill. Much of the Colvin Run Mill's gears and other machinery were handmade about 1811 from designs developed by Oliver Evans, the leading millwright-engineer of the early 19th century, whose designs were widely copied in Northern Virginia. This mill was typical of many along main thoroughfares which ground wheat and corn for neighborhood needs as well as the merchant trade in the ports of Alexandria, Georgetown and Baltimore. The Colvin Run Mill was rebuilt in the 1960s by the Fairfax County Park Authority. Courtesy of the photographer, Jack Hiller

In 1968, when Leesburg Pike was about to be widened by the Virginia Department of Highways, the Dranesville Tavern was moved off the right-of-way and was eventually restored by the Fairfax County Park Authority. Originally built in 1823 as a pair of log cabins connected by a breezeway, it was covered with weatherboard in the 1850s when additions were made. This tavern served all who traveled the turnpike, including the driver and passengers of the mail coach, the wagoner and his team, and the drover walking to market at the plodding pace of his animals. Animals being herded to market were kept overnight in pens back of the tavern. Courtesy of the artist, Gloria Matthews

In the early 19th century, turnpike companies constructed roads according to the methods of Englishman John McAdam, putting down layers of stones. Where stone was not readily available, a smooth-surface road could be made by putting down layers of logs and planks covered with dirt. In 1851, the Virginia General Assembly authorized construction of two plank roads from Fairfax Court House, one to Fairfax Station and one to Georgetown. Painting by Carl Rakeman, courtesy of the Federal Highway Administration

Captain Fountain Beattie, who served with Colonel John Mosby during the Civil War, posed with his wife, Anne Hathaway Beattie, at Green Spring Farm, which was their home from 1878 to 1917. Built by John Moss in 1760, the house became the centerpiece of Green Spring Garden Park after a portion of the farm was deeded in 1970 to the Fairfax County Park Authority by its last private owners, Michael and Belinda Straight. Green Spring Farm hosts special events including art and flower shows. The Park Authority has developed a notable horticultural center on the grounds.
Photograph courtesy of Elizabeth Buscher

Silas Burke is believed to have built this house about 1824, close to the time he married Hannah Coffer. He was born in Prince William County in 1796 and later became a prominent entrepreneur in Fairfax County, serving in many county offices, including chief justice of the county courts. He was a businessman and also served as a state director of both the Fairfax Turnpike Company and the Orange and Alexandria Railroad. The town of Burke was named for him. He died in 1854. Courtesy of the artist, Judith Pixton

Mount Vernon was beginning to deteriorate in 1853 when Ann Pamela Cunningham of South Carolina learned it was in a ruinous state and decided to do something about preserving the home of our nation's first president. She founded the Mount Vernon Ladies' Association of the Union in 1856, and by 1858, with the help of like-minded women throughout the nation, she had raised the $200,000 necessary to buy the estate. Miss Cunningham is shown here seated in a high-backed chair with a group of her vice regents. Still maintained by the Ladies' Association, Mount Vernon has the highest annual visitation of any historic house in the nation. Photograph in 1873, courtesy of the Mount Vernon Ladies' Association

The Friends of the Fairfax Station was founded in the early 1980s by Lena Wyckoff for the purpose of reconstructing the old Fairfax railroad station as a local community center and museum. After the participation of many individuals and organizations in the project, the building was dedicated in 1987 and a caboose was added to the station grounds in 1993. Courtesy of the photographer, Scott Boatright

A wintery hillside panorama shows the little village of Fairfax Station, as it appeared in 1916. It was the scene of Civil War action and especially the humanitarian activities of Clara Barton and her assistants with the thousands of wounded soldiers from the Second Battle of Manassas and the Battle of Ox Hill in 1862. The steeple of St. Mary's Church shows in the distance. The Catholic church had been established during the construction of the railroad as a place where railroad workers could worship. Courtesy of the artist, Ellen Jones

When Fairfax County celebrated the centennial anniversary of its public school system in 1970, one of the goals was to establish a school museum. The Legato School, shown here, was built about 1877, and as one of the few remaining one-room schools, it was moved from its original location on Route 29-211 to the 1800 Courthouse vicinity on Chain Bridge Road. Courtesy of the photographer, William Edmund Barrett

This two-story building was the first brick public school in Fairfax County; the first section was built in 1873. An addition was made on the front in 1912. In partnership with the City of Fairfax, Historic Fairfax City renovated the old school and opened the Fairfax Museum to the public on July 4, 1992. Courtesy of the Fairfax Museum and Visitor Center

Along the Potomac from the Occoquan River to Alexandria, at Great Hunting Creek, farm-to-market roads were in wretched condition for several decades following the devastation of the Civil War. One option available to Fairfax County farmers near the river was the use of river steamers such as the Mary Washington *shown in this advertisement. The historic Mount Vernon estate was also an excursion destination urged upon parents, teachers, guardians and children.* Courtesy of Fred Tilp

NEW LINE
AND
LOW FARE!!

THE NEW, LARGE AND ELEGANT STEAMER
MARY WASHINGTON,
M. E. GREGG, COMMANDER,

Will, until further notice, run as follows:

FARMERS' ACCOMMODATION

Will leave Accotink daily, Sundays excepted, at 6 a. m. precisely, for Alexandria and Washington, stopping at Gunston Hall, Whitehouse, Marshall Hall, Mount Vernon, Fort Washington and Collingwood.

MOUNT VERNON TRIP

For the accommodation of Excursionists, Pleasure Parties, Parents and Children, will leave Washington at 10 a. m. precisely, (city time) for Mount Vernon, giving the passengers ample time, not only to visit the Mansion and the Tomb, but all the classic grounds surrounding.

Fare from Washington and Alexandria to the new landing called "Mount Vernon Springs" and return. **ONLY FIFTY CENTS;** children under 12 years, half price. Parties visiting the Mount Vernon Mansion will be charged 25 cents extra for stage fare—one mile over an excellent and delightful road—and 25 cents, the admittance fee charged by the Mount Vernon Association.

Parents, Teachers and Guardians, bring out the little ones, and give them a safe and delightful trip on the new and commodious steamer to Mount Vernon Springs and the Tomb of Washington.

Returning to Accotink will leave Washington at 4 p. m., touching at all the intermediate landings.

The present Cherry Hill house was probably built about 1840. Joseph S. Riley, later a key figure in the incorporation of the town in 1875, acquired 80 acres of property and the house in 1870. When his son, Joseph Harvey Riley, a noted ornithologist, died in 1941, he willed the estate to the University of Virginia. The Falls Church City Council, through City Manager Harry Wells, purchased the property for a government enclave for city hall and community center buildings. The house and outbuildings have been restored and are maintained by the City. The Friends of Cherry Hill Foundation assists with periodic acquisitions and manages a docent program. Courtesy of the Falls Church Historical Commission

For a few months in 1898, during the Spanish-American War, Falls Church was the railroad station for nearby Camp Alger at Merrifield and its 23,000 troops in training for military service. Most visitors to the camp from Washington came by the trolley to East Falls Church and then proceeded to the camp on foot or by horse and buggy. Courtesy of the Falls Church Historical Commission

Brown's Hardware is a family business which celebrated its 100th anniversary in 1983. James W. Brown came to Falls Church from Loudoun County and established a store selling groceries, hardware, paint, oils and glass. His son, Horace Brown, Sr., took over the business in 1904, and his son Hugh owned the store from the 1950s. In 1959, a modern one-story building on the adjacent lot became Brown's Hardware. Courtesy of the Mary Riley Styles Public Library, Falls Church

Edwin Bancroft Henderson was throughout his long and productive adult life engaged in working for equality and justice under the law for black citizens. He was a physical training teacher and basketball coach in Washington public schools following his graduation from Howard and Columbia universities. In 1910, he and his wife Mary Ellen moved to Falls Church. His wife became a teacher and then principal at the James Lee Elementary School. He was author of two books about African-American athletes. Harris & Ewing photograph, courtesy of the Falls Church Historical Commission

The Tinner Hill monument was dedicated in June 1999. It commemorates contributions made by E. B. Henderson and Joseph Tinner in 1915 in founding the nation's first rural chapter of the National Association for the Advancement of Colored People, at Falls Church. Courtesy of the photographer, Scott Boatright

The residents of Clifton, Virginia, have heard the sound of trains rolling through their town since the establishment of the town, which was platted by the county supervisors in 1869 at the site of Devereux Station. Large quantities of wood were shipped from this location for the use of the Union Army during the Civil War. Courtesy of the artist, Ellen Jones

In the 1840s, Matthew Fontaine Maury, superintendent of the U. S. Department of Charts and Instruments, directed Captain William Lewis Herndon to explore the Amazon River for its entire length. After Captain Herndon went down with his ship, the Central America, *in a storm off Cape Hatteras in 1857, the village fathers decided to honor the dead hero. They named their new postal village "Herndon" in 1858. The town was incorporated in 1879 under the same name.* Courtesy of the Library of Virginia

This funeral procession was on the way to Herndon's Chestnut Grove Cemetery about 1900. It is one of more than 200 historical Herndon photographs in the collection of the late J. Berkley Green, many of them on display in the Green Funeral Home. Courtesy of J. Berkley Green

There has been a depot in the same place since the Alexandria, Loudoun & Hampshire Railroad was built through Herndon in 1859. In the 1890s, the Southern Railway absorbed this and other railroad lines into its large system. The Herndon Historical Society established a museum in the old town depot in 1971. It acquired a red caboose in 1989.
Photograph by Ross Netherton

The old Vienna Library, built in 1897, was moved to the side yard of the Freeman house and store in 1969. The Freeman house was probably built in 1859 and has served at various times as a residence, store, post office, insurance office and a garage for the town's first fire truck. The Town of Vienna purchased the property in 1969. Nearby on the Washington & Old Dominion Bike/Hike Trail is a red caboose. Photograph by Ross Netherton

The Vienna Railroad Station was probably remodeled in 1894 after the Southern Railway took over the Washington, Ohio & Western Railroad. The last train ran in 1968 and subsequently the tracks were removed. When the Virginia Electric & Power Company purchased the right-of-way from what had become the Washington & Old Dominion Railroad, the power company gave the station to the Town of Vienna. It is currently leased as a clubhouse by the Northern Virginia Model Railroaders, Inc. From the postcard collection of Tony Chaves

For 26 years, Louise Reeves Archer commuted from her home in Washington to Vienna, first by trolley and train, and then by automobile, to serve as fifth-to-seventh grade teacher and principal at the Vienna Colored School. She believed strongly in the value of a formal education. When Mrs. Archer died unexpectedly in 1948, parents and students petitioned the school board to change the school's name to honor her. This was done in 1950. The school was integrated in 1959 along with other county public schools. Courtesy of Fairfax County Library Photographic Archive

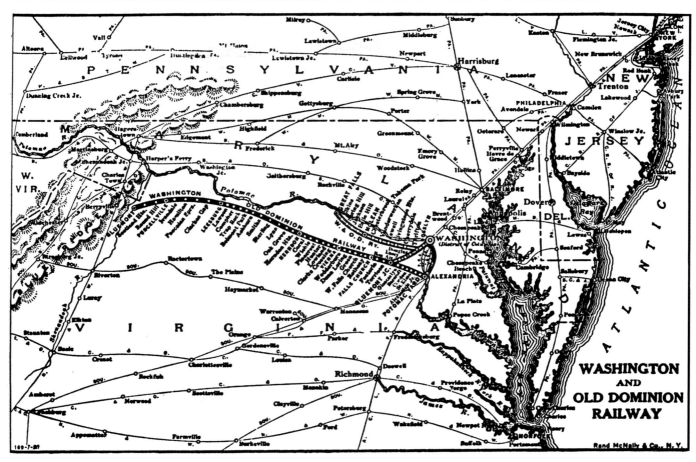

The Alexandria, Loudoun & Hampshire Railroad was organized in Northern Virginia in 1853. After the Civil War, the ownership and name changed several times. Known for a while after 1894 as the Bluemont Branch of the Southern Railway, it was leased by the Southern in 1912 and renamed the Washington & Old Dominion Railway. The railroad was abandoned by court order in 1968 and the tracks were removed. The right-of-way is now used by Virginia Power for transmission lines and managed as a linear bike-hike park by the Northern Virginia Regional Park Authority. Map courtesy of Rand McNally & Company

The branch of the Washington and Old Dominion Railway which terminated at Great Falls on the Potomac and the large inn there made the park an ideal location for retreats, meetings, and conferences. Shown here is a group of ministers gathered at Great Falls in 1910 for the annual Camp Meeting and Biblical Institute of the Methodist Church. Courtesy of the Fairfax County Library Photographic Archive

The Fairfax Chapter of the Daughters of the American Revolution met in 1912 to place a bronze plaque on a large stone in Great Falls Park. The text honored George Washington, patriot, pioneer, and man of affairs, for the building of the Patowmack Canal, by the company of which he was the first president. Courtesy of the Fairfax County Library Photographic Archive

To humble beginnings of privately funded community libraries, Fairfax County added a borrowed bookmobile in 1940 to carry about 600 books on regularly scheduled trips through rural neighborhoods. In 1953, a professional librarian, Mary K. McCulloch, was hired to build a county-wide system. The system has repeatedly recorded the largest annual circulation figures of any library in the South. Courtesy of Fairfax County Library Photographic Archive

This country dirt road in Fairfax County was captured in a tranquil moment in May 1941 by professional photographer Marion Post Wolcott. It was part of an effort to record the rural character and appearance of farmland of that period by the Farm Security Administration under the U. S. Department of Agriculture. Courtesy of the Library of Congress

In the 1880s, telephone exchanges were established in Falls Church, Fairfax, Vienna, Herndon and in the neighboring cities and counties of Loudoun, Fauquier and Prince William. Dr. M. E. Church, a pharmacist and entrepreneur in Falls Church, provided additional telephone and telegraph service to Camp Alger in 1898. In 1916, the Chesapeake & Potomac Telephone Company bought the utility. Photograph from the 1940s. Courtesy of Falls Church Historical Commission

This view of a grocery store near Falls Church in the mid-1950s shows the standard response of merchants of the time to the need for customer parking. The growing population led to the building of suburban shopping centers and malls in Fairfax County starting in 1953, where a central parking area could serve a number of shops. Porter photograph, courtesy of Fairfax County Library Photographic Archive

During World War II, in conjunction with the building of the Pentagon in Arlington, Shirley Memorial Highway was constructed, named to honor Henry G. Shirley, Virginia State Highway Commissioner from 1922 to 1941. When the first section opened in 1944 between the Pentagon and Route 7, Leesburg Pike, it ushered in the express-way era of highway travel in Northern Virginia. Courtesy of Virginia Department of Transportation

Robert E. Simon purchased 7,000 acres of western Fairfax County land in 1961 to develop a carefully planned community – an innovative "New Town." Successor developers were Gulf Oil and Mobil Oil. Numerous high technology companies have established handsome campuses throughout Reston, and employment, educational, residential, and recreational opportunities abound. The 2000 population of Reston was approximately 55,000. Portrait courtesy of Hunters Woods Library

In 1973, the national headquarters of the United States Geological Survey were moved to Reston as part of the federal government's effort to decentralize many of its agencies. The buildings, designed in the shape of a mapmaker's traditional compass rose, provide a million square feet of floor space for the world's largest earth science library, modern geological and hydrological laboratories and a topographic mapping plant. Courtesy of Reston Land Corporation

In 1966, Mrs. Jouett Shouse gave 95 acres of woods and meadows near Vienna to the National Park Service to establish the nation's first national park for the performing arts. An outdoor theater was built, with seating for 7,500 people inside and outside on the lawn. Two 200-year old barns, one of German design and other English, were moved from Pennsylvania to form the Barns of Wolf Trap which are mainly in use during the winter months for varied programs. Courtesy of the Wolf Trap Foundation

John Jackson lived on Ox Road in Fairfax Station but he had been all over the world as one of the globe's premier blues and country guitarists. Born in Rappahannock County to a music-loving family, he learned to play the guitar and banjo when a small boy. He and his wife Cora Lee moved to Fairfax where he worked on a farm. He was "discovered" by folklorist Chuck Perdue of the University of Virginia in 1964. He entertained audiences in most of the major countries of the world and knew 600-700 songs. His son, James, or his friend, Bill McGinnis, often played with him on local music dates. John Jackson died in January 2002. Courtesy of the photographer, Larry Daniels

VII

Loudoun County

Loudoun County was formed from the northwestern part of Fairfax County in 1757, but its boundaries were redrawn to their present locations in 1798. The county was named for John Campbell, fourth Earl of Loudoun, who commanded the British forces in North America from 1756 to 1759. He also was Governor of Virginia during these years, but never visited Virginia and was represented by his deputy, Lieutenant Governor Robert Dinwiddie.

Settlement of what was to become Loudoun County began between 1720 and 1730 while the area was part of Prince William County. Although the Church of England was the established church in Virginia and the new county was divided into parishes, dissenters were allowed to hold services and follow their own tenets provided they registered their preaching points and the location of their church buildings. Members of the Society of Friends, familiarly known as Quakers, came from Pennsylvania to settle in the Waterford and Leesburg areas. Their communities were characterized by their freedom of religious and moral thought, their advanced farming practices, which made the county's good soil yield abundant harvests, and the wholesome society they fostered.

During the mid-eighteenth century German settlers from Pennsylvania and New York, refugees from the almost constant wars of central Europe, generally kept their own native languages, habits, customs and traditions. Their tightly-knit communities in the northwestern parts of the county were well organized for defense in the frontier Indian wars of the late eighteenth century. Settlers of English ancestry moved into Loudoun County from the Tidewater areas as soon as they could acquire the means to do so, and their farms were in the Middleburg area and along the Potomac River and its tributaries.

Even before the French and Indian wars subsided, however, Aeneas Campbell began to build a county courthouse in 1758 on land acquired from Nicholas Minor, who owned an ordinary in the settlement then called "George Town." The community which grew up around the courthouse became the county seat with the name of Leesburg.

James Monroe's home in Loudoun, Oak Hill, is on a hilltop overlooking the Carolina Road (Rte. 15) and the Oatlands estate across from it. Here Monroe and much of the county's population were hosts when General Lafayette visited the United States in 1824-25.

In 1853, Yardley Taylor, a Quaker serving as county surveyor at the time, drew the first detailed map of the county. On it were the locations of various natural features and resources, mills, roads, villages and towns, all information essential for travelers of that time.

As war clouds gathered in 1861, the county was divided in its allegiances. Two companies of local soldiers, called the Loudoun Rangers, were raised to serve with the Union army, but secession sentiment was strong and widespread.

For almost a century after the end of the Civil War, Loudoun residents continued to farm the land and sell their agricultural produce in the Baltimore, Washington and Richmond markets. Farmers' clubs, especially the Grange organization, encouraged better husbandry for improved strains of plants and animals, and restoration of productivity by fertilization of soils.

The increased mobility provided by better roads, automobiles and trucks following World War II, and the greater employment opportunities in and around the county eventually ended the agricultural economy and country life style of Loudoun County. Construction of Dulles International Airport and the Capital Beltway in the 1960s led to construction of residential subdivisions. Shopping malls, offices, business and professional services, and offices of local, state and federal government have followed. Pressure for more transportation facilities, recreational amenities, and housing have arisen to serve the growth that continues.

Thus, Loudoun is a county in transition. Parts are experiencing impacts of urbanization as the County's population has increased from 18,962 in 1790 to 169,599 in 2000.

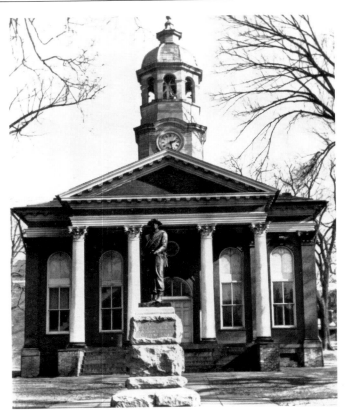

The Loudoun County Courthouse shown here was built on the same site as two previous courthouses and was opened for court business in 1894. Its unusual architectural style features tall white columns topped with Corinthian capitols, a rooftop cupola, and a clock. On the approach to the front, a statue of a Confederate soldier stands upon a rough-hewn granite block, in which is mounted a plaque listing the county's veterans of World War I. This monument was designed by William Sebier, who was also sculptor of The Virginia Group at the Gettysburg Battlefield in Pennsylvania. Courtesy of the Arlington Public Library

Loudoun County, formed by the Virginia Assembly from the northern part of Fairfax County in 1757, was named after John Campbell, fourth Earl of Loudoun, who was governor of Virginia from 1756 to 1759. Campbell was appointed commander-in-chief of British forces in America, but because military action did not go well, he was removed from his position. Benjamin Franklin remarked that the Earl was "Like St. George on the signs, always on horseback and never rides on." Portrait courtesy of the Loudoun Museum

Once called Goose Creek, the present-day village of Lincoln was settled by Quakers in the mid-18th century. The Goose Creek Meeting House complex at Lincoln consists of three buildings and a Quaker burial ground on the edge of the little village. The 1765 stone meeting house shown here became a residence. Courtesy of the Virginia Department of Historic Resources

A horse, with rider and hounds, moves past the Woodburn Plantation, built in the second quarter of the 19th century. A log patent house on the estate may also date to 1777. Located four miles from Leesburg off Route 15, the complex is of particular importance because all of its numerous main buildings have been preserved. Courtesy of the Arlington Public Library

The first land deeded to the Methodist Church in America was the lot in Leesburg on which the stone church shown here was built by 1790. The Old Stone Church site including its grave-yard has been landscaped and marked as an official National Historic Shrine of the United Methodist Church. Photograph taken in 1892. From the postcard collection of Tony Chaves

Belmont, a Georgian brick house outside of Leesburg, was built by Ludwell Lee in 1797. He was the son of Richard Henry Lee and Anne Aylett Lee of Westmoreland County. After Lee's death in 1836, Belmont was sold to Margaret Mercer, who opened a school for girls. Belmont became the property of International Business Machines in 1968. Courtesy of the Loudoun Museum

The building of the Oatlands mansion was begun in 1804 by George Carter, son of Robert Carter of Nomini Hall. It is one of the finest Federal estates in the nation with numerous out-buildings and fine formal gardens. The Oatlands Historic District encompasses the estate and other sites and structures including the archaeological site of Oatlands Mills, a village church and parish hall, and the Mountain Gap School, a rural one-room 19th century school-house painted red. Closed in 1953, the school became a museum. Courtesy of the Library of Virginia

President James Monroe began construction of his retire-ment home, Oak Hill, in Loudoun County while he was still serving as chief executive of the United States. The build-ing was possibly designed by Thomas Jefferson and James Hoban. When President John Quincy Adams and General Lafayette paid a three-day visit to Monroe at Oak Hill in 1825, 10,000 spectators gathered nearby to greet and honor them at what has been called "the greatest social event in the his-tory of Leesburg." Courtesy of the Library of Virginia

The Aldie Mill was begun in 1807 by Charles Fenton Mercer. It had two wooden mill wheels allowing for extensive output of grain products and other materials. Charles Fenton Mercer was one of the organizers of the Goose Creek and Little River Navigation Company in 1839. Aldie was laid out on his land and was named for the Mercer family castle in Scotland. Painting courtesy of the Douglas family

The early 19th century bridge which carries Route 50, the Little River Turnpike, over the Little River at Aldie is the last remaining such bridge still in use in Virginia which dates from the turnpike era. From Aldie, the Ashby Gap Turnpike was authorized in 1810 by the Virginia Assembly, extending a roadway to Snickersville (Bluemont) and the Blue Ridge. Photograph by Edward Breitenbach, courtesy of the Arlington Public Library

Built before 1817 on property in Waterford sold by Jonas Potts to Emanuel Newcomer in that year, the brick house on the hill was purchased by the Walker family in 1859 and owned by them for over 60 years. Its owners have granted a perpetual easement to the Virginia Department of Historic Resources to protect Mill End, the Federal-style house, from inappropriate change. Courtesy of the Library of Virginia

The Poor House Farm

Ellen Jones

In 1822, Loudoun's nine Overseers of the Poor purchased the county's third poorhouse farm located near Middleburg in the shadow of the Blue Ridge. There was a stone in the south gable marked W.B. 1814 by the builder, William Burson. After use as an efficiently run "alms house" for more than a century, the farm was sold by the county in 1946. In recent years, the Poor House Farm became a Virginia Hunt Country bed and breakfast establishment. Drawing courtesy of the artist, Ellen Jones

During the 1700s, at least six ferries crossed the Potomac River in Loudoun County. Only one remains on the entire Potomac, White's Ferry, once known as Conrad's Ferry, probably established in 1828. Off Route 15 north of Leesburg on Route 655, it operates every day except when the river freezes or floods. The ferry was named for nearby White's Ford where Confederate General Jubal Early crossed the Potomac on July 14, 1864 on his way to threaten the city of Washington.
Early 1900s photo courtesy of the Arlington County Public Library

Originally known as Snickersville, the little community was named after a family who operated a Shenandoah River ferry in the valley below on the western side of the Blue Ridge Mountains. At the suggestion of the Southern Railway, which terminated this particular branch at Snickersville, the residents agreed to change the name to Bluemont in 1900 to make the hamlet more attractive to tourists as a summer resort. From the postcard collection of Tony Chaves

Westmoreland Davis, of Morven Park in Loudoun County, was governor of Virginia from 1918 to 1922. He came to Virginia in 1903 with his wife, the former Marguerite Inman of Georgia. At Morven Park, Davis plunged into scientific farming, helped organize the Virginia Dairymen's Association, and became president of the Farmers' Institute. The portrait of Davis as "The Master of Hounds," painted around 1900 by F. T. Wild, appeared on the cover of the January 1938 edition of The Southern Planter, *which Davis took over in 1909.* Courtesy of the Library of Congress

Born at Burrland, Charlotte Haxall Noland was descended from four notable families of Loudoun County. She decided early in her own educational experience that she would one day have a school of her own where girls could enjoy learning. "Miss Charlotte" bought the Locust Lane property near Middleburg and opened Foxcroft School there in 1914. By the late 1940s, Foxcroft was rated academically among the top ten girls' schools in the country. Portrait courtesy of Foxcroft School

Incorporated in 1908, the town of Purcellville is on land believed to have been first settled by James Dillon in the mid-18th century. An ordinary was opened on the road that ran from Snickers Gap to Leesburg around 1800, operated by Abraham and Sarah Vickers. Edgar Rodney Purcell operated a store from 1847 to 1892, serving as postmaster for 26 years. The photograph of the Purcellville School Fair Parade was taken by C. R. Ward of Purcellville in May 1915. From the postcard collection of Tony Chaves

Frances Reid was born in Hume, Virginia and was raised by her uncle and aunt in Purcellville. She began working for the Loudoun Times-Mirror in 1921 and eventually became a columnist and editor. With her ancient Royal typewriter, she pounded out the local news for 71 years. At 86 years of age, she published her book about the history of Loudoun County newspapers entitled Inside Loudoun: The Way It Was. She retired from the paper in 1992.
Photograph by Victoria J. Bellerose, courtesy of the *Loudoun Times-Mirror*

In 1922 a brick library was built with funds from the Balch family to honor Thomas Balch, an international jurist and author. Initially a private subscription library, it became a public library about 1960. When the new Leesburg Library building was completed in 1991, the Thomas Balch Library became a local history branch for historical and genealogical research of Loudoun County and the Northern Virginia area. From the postcard collection of Tony Chaves

George Catlett Marshall (1880-1959) was born in Uniontown, Pennsylvania, educated at the Virginia Military Institute, class of 1901. He called Leesburg his home from 1941 to 1959, living with his family at historic Dodona Manor. During this time he served as U. S. Army Chief of Staff with rank of General of the Armies, as Secretary of State, as President of the Red Cross, and as Secretary of Defense. He received the Nobel Peace Prize in 1953. This life-size statue was designed by sculptor Rosario R. Fiore in 1976. Courtesy of the photographer, Richard Netherton

Dulles International Airport was completed in 1962 on land in both Fairfax and Loudoun counties. The control tower, terminal, service buildings and mobile lounges were designed by Eero Saarinen and considered by him to be his best architectural accomplishment. The airport was officially named after Secretary of State John Foster Dulles, who served in the Eisenhower administration. Courtesy of Arlington County Public Library

The nation's early exploration of outer space is remembered by a space shuttle and the capsules from rocket-launched flights now preserved in the Udvar-Hazy Center of the Smithsonian Institution's National Air and Space Museum at Dulles Airport. Photograph by Ross Netherton

The Loudoun Museum was founded by a group of business people in Loudoun in April 1977. Through the coopera- tive efforts of Loudoun County and the town of Leesburg, the museum serves as a history museum and a tourist informa- tion center for the region. Over 16,000 visitors per year, both domestic and foreign, enjoy the museum's exhibits, lectures, con- certs, receptions and private previews. Courtesy of the photogra- pher, Richard Netherton

Henry Taylor of Lincoln re- ceived a Pulitzer Prize in 1986 for his book of poetry, The Flying Change. A lifelong resident of Loudoun whose forebears in the area go back two centuries, Taylor's poetry reflects the life around him. The poet studied at the University of Virginia. Photograph by Sandra Ehrenkrane, cour- tesy of the Thomas Balch Library

Near the courthouse in Warrenton is the old brick jail, built in 1808. Behind it is a stone jail which began use in 1823 when the brick building became the jailer's residence. Prisoners were housed in the stone jail until 1966. Since 1975 the Fauquier County Historical Society has operated a museum in the two buildings. Photograph by Ruth Rose

VIII

Fauquier County

In 1759 the southwestern portion of Prince William County was removed for governmental purposes to become a new county, named in honor of Francis Fauquier, who had become Virginia's Lieutenant Governor one year earlier. The county's first court session met near Morrisville in May 1759. Seven different courthouses have since been constructed.

On the eve of the American Revolution, Fauquier County, together with neighboring Culpeper and Orange Counties, raised a regiment of 350 men for service. Popularly known as the Culpeper Minute Men, it once was characterized by John Randolph of Roanoke as "raised in a minute, armed in a minute, marched in a minute, fought in a minute, and vanished in a minute." But it served honorably and reflected the strong sentiment for independence in the central Piedmont section of Virginia.

In 1777, a classical school was opened near Fauquier Court House by Princeton graduate Hezekiah Balch, and named the Warren Academy honoring the hero of the Battle of Bunker Hill in Boston. Also, in 1803 the Warren Masonic Lodge was established at the courthouse. Thus it was not surprising for the General Assembly in 1810 to select Warrenton as the name for a new town established in the county.

The town's location was advantageous for farmers of the area when shipping their agricultural produce to the markets in Alexandria and the District of Columbia, and in the 1820s a turnpike road was built from Warrenton to connect with the Little River Turnpike at Fairfax Court House.

Fauquier County's economy remained firmly planted in the rich soil of the Piedmont, and later in the nine-teenth century when the focus on wheat and associated grains shifted to the Mid-West and Great Plains, Fauquier's "blue grass" soil produced good forage for thoroughbred horses and purebred cattle. Today Fauquier's economy and style of life still reflect its rural character while at the same time accommodating the needs of a regional transportation corridor.

The Upperville Horse Show, which began in 1853, still is an annual event. Steeplechasing and point-to-point horse racing go on most of the year. The county has five recognized fox hunting clubs. In Victorian times, Fauquier's White Sulphur Springs was a fashionable spa, known for the scenic beauty of its setting and its entertainment as well as the medicinal quality of the water.

As twentieth century travel shifted to rails and highways, threats to the traditional beauty of the Blue Ridge and Shenandoah Valley led to interest in its preservation. Polly (Mrs. Samuel A.) Appleton of Warrenton urged women to join in the promotion of gardening and highway roadside beautification. The first such organization in Virginia and the third in the country was the Warrenton Garden Club, formed in 1911. It was a founding member of the Garden Club of America in 1913 and Garden Club of Virginia in 1920.

Preservation of Fauquier County's historic buildings and records is promoted by the Fauquier Historical Society, established in 1965, the Fauquier Heritage Society, formed in 1993, and the Afro-American Society, organized in 1992.

Fauquier County in 2000 remains mainly rural, its population having increased from 17,892 in 1790 to 55,139 in 2000.

Francis Fauquier was appointed lieutenant governor of Virginia in 1758 and served until his death in 1768. He possessed many traits which enhanced his official service during the unsettled times prior to the American Revolution. He had a scientific mind, was musical, humane, polished and genuinely interested in Virginia and its people. Portrait courtesy of John K. Gott

Six courthouses have been built since Fauquier County was formed in 1759. The third courthouse was constructed on the present site in 1795. The 1854 courthouse burned in 1889 because of a "grand jollification at Warrenton as a result of the recent Democratic victory," when festivities included fireworks and a bonfire in the courthouse lot. It was replaced in 1890. Behind the courthouse is the old jail, constructed in 1822 and later operated as a museum by the Fauquier Historical Society, which was established in 1965. This 1900 view is from the postcard collection of Tony Chaves

John Marshall was born in 1755 in a house on Licking Run near Germantown. He was admitted to the bar in 1780, became a member of the General Assembly of Virginia and the United States Congress. He served as Secretary of State under President John Adams. He was appointed Chief Justice of the Supreme Court of the United States in 1801 and served in that capacity until his death in 1835. His Fauquier County home from 1773 on, was Oak Hill. The portrait shown is a copy of the original posthumous painting by William D. Washington for the Fauquier County Courthouse in 1859. Courtesy of the National Archives

Fauquier White Sulphur Springs near Warrenton, once known as Lee's Sulphur, is situated only about 50 miles west of Washington and guests flocked there from the capital and from Alexandria. Fauquier Springs offered horse racing, hunting hounds and steeds, a ball every night and games of bowls and quoits. But by far the most popular entertainment was the tournament. Lithograph made in 1857, courtesy of Arlington Public Library

French American Revolutionary War General Marie Joseph Paul Ives Roch Gilbert du Motier, the Marquis de Lafayette, returned to the United States on a farewell tour as "The Nation's Guest" in 1824 and 1825. Lafayette was a guest at Warrenton in August 1825, accompanied by former President James Monroe, Congressman Charles Fenton Mercer and other dignitaries, in open carriages. The Fauquier Cavalry, the United States Marine Band from Washington, D. C., and 5,000 to 6,000 spectators took part in or observed the parade held in his honor on Main Street. Painting of Lafayette about 1824, courtesy of the Library of Congress

General Lafayette had so endeared himself to the citizens of Warrenton during his farewell tour in 1825 that upon the report of his death, the town prepared a special ceremony which took place on July 12, 1834. This copy of a printed broadside, "Honors to the memory of Lafayette," shows the order of Lafayette's memorial procession at Warrenton.
Courtesy of the National Museum of American History, Smithsonian Institution

HONORS TO THE MEMORY OF LAFAYETTE.

The Marshal appointed to conduct the procession in in honor of General LAFAYETTE,on Saturday, the 12th July, at Warrenton, has adopted the following order: The procession will be formed in front of the Court-house, at 11 o'clock precisely ; the Military are to parade at 10 o'clock, and hold themselves in readiness to join the procession without delay ; the citizens who intend to unite in the procession, are respectfully requested to assemble in order at 11 o'clock, when the whole will be formed in the following order :

UNIFORM COMPANIES OF MILITIA.
COMPANIES NOT IN UNIFORM.
CLERGY.
REVOLUTIONARY OFFICERS AND SOLDIERS.
OFFICERS OF THE U. S. ARMY & NAVY.
MILITIA OFFICERS IN UNIFORM.
JUDGES, MEMBERS OF THE BAR, CLERKS AND SHERIFFS.
MAGISTRATES OF THE COUNTY.
HEADS OF SCHOOLS AND THEIR PUPILS.
MASONIC FRATERNITY.
CITIZENS, *four a breast.*
CAVALRY.
CITIZENS *on Horseback and in Carriages.*

The procession, thus formed, will march to the Brick Church and halt until the Citizens have entered the church, when the Military will proceed, in order, to occupy the Galleries. After the ceremonies in the church are over, the procession will be formed in like manner and marched to the public square and dismissed.

The following gentlemen are requested to act as assistant Marshals :

Capt. LUTHER SULLIVAN,§ Capt. THOS, T. FAUNTLEROY,
" WM. W. WALLACE, § " HENRY H. WITHERS,
" WM. S. KEMPER, § " THOS. R. HAMPTON.

JOHN WALDEN,
Marshal.

July 7, 1834

Printed at the INDEPENDENT REGISTER Office

Melrose Castle, sometimes called Castle Murray, was constructed between 1856 and 1860 near Casanova by builder George Washington Holtzclaw for two brothers, James and Edward Murray. Mary Roberts Rinehart found inspiration from it for her popular mystery novel, The Circular Staircase. *This photograph was taken by T. N. O'Sullivan in November 1863, when Federal troops occupied the Melrose property during the Civil War.* Courtesy of the National Archives

Oakley, completed in 1857 in the Upperville area, is a residence in the Italian villa design. Its first owner was Henry Grafton Dulany, founder of the Upperville Colt and Horse Show, the oldest organization of its kind in the country. During the Civil War, the house was occupied first by Confederate and then by Union troops. Courtesy of the Virginia Department of Historic Resources

The Fauquier County Courthouse is shown between the former County Clerk's office, on the left, and the California Building, on the right. The 19th century brick building was constructed for use as a residence by William "Extra Billy" Smith, who was twice elected governor of Virginia. These buildings are part of the Warrenton Historic District.
Courtesy of the *Fauquier Times-Democrat*

An early and enthusiastic advocate of physical fitness, President Theodore Roosevelt challenged military men and government officials to a day's ride of 100 miles round trip to Warrenton from Washington, D. C., in blustery cold weather. Large numbers of townspeople turned out to welcome him and his party and to feed them lunch. In appreciation, Roosevelt later sent them a copy of this full-length portrait of himself in hunting clothes painted by Northern Virginia artist Gari Melchers at the White House in 1908.
Courtesy of the Freer Gallery of Art, Smithsonian Instution, Washington, D. C.
Gift of Charles Lang Freer, F1908.17

Waverly is a 300-acre dairy farm with a stone house, a portion of which was constructed in the 1790s by Charles Chinn, who then owned the property. In 1973, at the age of 75, owner Mrs. Thomas F. Furness started the Piedmont Vineyards on 30 acres of the farm, becoming a pioneer in the wine industry in Virginia. Courtesy of the Virginia Department of Historic Resources

Philanthropist and patron of the arts Paul Mellon was born in Pittsburgh, Pennsylvania. He lived at Oak Spring in Fauquier County, where he raised race horses. His many gifts to the Commonwealth of Virginia and the nation included an addition to the National Gallery of Art, the East Building, designed by architect I. M. Pei, and built in 1978. Photograph of Paul Mellon riding Red Reef in 1979 taken by Marshall Hawkins. Courtesy of the *Fauquier Times-Democrat*

Included in the Upperville Historic District, established in 1972 along Route 50, is the Trinity Episcopal Church. Built in the style of a French medieval parish church, it was a gift to the congregation in the 1950s by Mr. and Mrs. Paul Mellon. Photograph by Jim Corbett, courtesy of the Virginia Chamber of Commerce

Taken in 1990, this informal portrait includes (seated) Wendy and Tom Arundel; (standing, left to right) Don, Sally Arundel, and Margaret DeWees; and Peggy, Arthur W., John and Peter Arundel. Arthur W. Arundel is founder and president of ArCom, Inc., which publishes 18 local weekly papers in Northern Virginia. Since 1980, ArCom newspapers have won hundreds of awards from the Virginia Press Association. Mr. Arundel has also been involved in a number of conservation activities, established the steeplechase course at Great Meadows, and has had a key role in the revitalization of The Plains, Virginia. Courtesy of ArCom, Inc.

Artist-blacksmith Nol Putnam is shown making a fork on his German pattern anvil at the White Oak Forge in The Plains, Virginia. He designs most of the work he creates, including three gates for columbaria (burial vaults) of the Washington National Cathedral. Behind Mr. Putnam is a coal-fired forge and a few of the myriad tools which he has made or collected over the years. Courtesy of the photographer, Richard Netherton

One of the memorial gates made at White Oak Forge in The Plains by Nol Putnam for the Washington National Cathedral, Mount St. Albans, in Washington, D. C. was completed in 1993. Courtesy of the photographer, Henry Eastwood

Symbolizing the abrupt transition from a small commercial riverside village to a modern multi-use urban center, this silk screen print by Margaret Fisher in 1964 shows the structural steel of new high-rise office buildings under construction in Rosslyn engulfing a small country-style church which was soon razed. Courtesy of the artist and the Arlington Historical Society

IX

Arlington County

Arlington is the smallest county in Virginia (25.6 square miles). When the United States became independent, Arlington was part of Fairfax County. Then, in 1800, it became part of the District of Columbia. It acquired county status in 1847 when the Virginia General Assembly formally accepted the Federal government's legislation organizing it into a separate county. In this way, "Alexandria County, District of Columbia" became "Alexandria County, Virginia." The town of Alexandria was included in this territory and served as the county seat.

During the Civil War (1861-65) and Reconstruction (1865-70) the county was occupied by Federal forces. In 1870, local government entered a new stage as the state government underwent basic constitutional changes and Alexandria became a separate city. The small county area which had been an economic appendage of Alexandria and Washington City began to develop its own community personality and the political institutions of a separate county. This process went on from 1870 to 1898, and the area became a patchwork of neighborhoods and corporate villages which had to learn from experience how to identify its common interests and how to cooperate in achieving them. The end of this period was symbolized by construction of a new courthouse, centrally located with space to grow as the county prospered.

Following this period, the county achieved individuality in several ways. Its name was changed to avoid confusion with neighboring Alexandria City and the name of "Arlington County" was adopted in 1920. Thus it honored its most famous landmark, Arlington House. Also, pursuant to legislation by the Virginia General Assembly in 1930, it became the first county in the state to adopt a County Manager form of government in 1932.

As Arlington County developed separately from the District of Columbia, its numerous communities and villages began to organize to improve the lives of their citizens. The Good Citizens League began a campaign in the early 1900s to rid the county of undesirable businesses. Citizens associations were formed in Cherrydale, Fort Myer Heights, Ballston, the Alexandria Courthouse area, Clarendon, Parkway and other communities. By 1914, the Alexandria Civic Federation had been formed and was urging the Board of Supervisors to develop a system of highways and streets. As the county's population grew at the time of the Second World War, facilities which had satisfied the needs of a rural, sparsely settled county no longer were adequate, and new countywide organizations promoted the building of schools and other facilities to meet their growing needs.

A major aspect of Arlington County's growth in the last half of the twentieth century has been the presence of Federal facilities within the county. Part of this trend has been the decentralization of government agencies formerly concentrated in the city of Washington. Part has been the location in Arlington of things having historical as well as functional value. A list would include Arlington National Cemetery, the Pentagon, Fort Myer, the George Washington Memorial Parkway, Arlington Memorial Bridge, and many monuments that have become major tourist attractions.

Arlington County, with a rich heritage of history to share, continues to grow and serve as the Potomac Gateway to Northern Virginia. In 1850 Arlington (then Alexandria County) had a population of 10,008, and in 2000 Arlington County's population was 189,453.

Arlington House from a sketch made about 1891 emphasizes the monumental quality of its architecture. The mansion was built on the 1,100 acre estate of George Washington Parke Custis, using brick of clay on the site and timber from its forests. The site overlooking the Potomac River and City of Washington originally was called Mount Washington. It was re-named "Arlington" after the Custis family's seat in Northampton County on Virginia's eastern shore. Courtesy of the National Park Service

The Alexandria County courthouse tower and central block were built about 1898, near the present Wilson Boulevard, between Rosslyn and Clarendon. This photograph was taken in the 1930s after one wing had been added. A successor courthouse building was constructed across the street and dedicated 1995. Courtesy of the Library of Virginia

John Ball received a 166-acre grant from Lord Fairfax in 1742 and became one of the first settlers in the area of the present-day Glencarlyn community, near Four Mile Run. The log portion of the Ball-Sellers house, the oldest documented dwelling remaining in Arlington County, was probably built between 1742 and 1750. The early shingle roof of the house remains in place under the exterior roof. Sketch by Rudolph Wendelin, courtesy of the artist and the Arlington Historical Society

BALL HOMESTEAD - 1767

The boundaries of what was to become the Federal District of Columbia were surveyed in 1791 in a square, ten miles to each side, with boundary stones set at approximately one-mile intervals. In 1976, the Department of the Interior placed the southwest #9 boundary stone in Arlington on the National Register of Historic Places and designated it a National Historic Landmark named after Benjamin Banneker, a black mathematician and inventor who was a member of the 1791 surveying team. Courtesy of the photographer, Richard Netherton

George Washington Parke Custis was the grandson of Martha Dandridge Custis Washington and was raised by the Washingtons at Mount Vernon. He built the grand mansion at Arlington, named it after an old Custis estate on the Eastern Shore and practiced scientific farming on his estate. He married Mary Lee Fitzhugh of Ravensworth. Pencil sketch by J. Kayler in 1852, courtesy of Arlington House

Mary Anna Randolph Custis Lee sat for this daguerreotype about 1845 with one of her children. Mrs. Lee was the wife of Gen. Robert E. Lee, whom she married in 1831, and the great-granddaughter of Martha Washington, wife of George Washington. Courtesy of the Virginia Historical Society

Robert Edward Lee was born in 1807 at Stratford Hall, in Westmoreland County, Virginia. He was a son of "Light Horse Harry" Lee and Anne Hill Carter, and grew up in Alexandria. After graduation in 1829 from the U. S. Military Academy, he served in the U. S. Army until the Civil War began. Lee eventually became general in chief of all the Confederate armies and therefore, in defeat, surrendered to Union General U. S. Grant at Appomattox on April 9, 1865. Lee served as president of Washington College in Lexington, Virginia from 1865 until his death in 1870. The school was then renamed Washington and Lee University. Courtesy of the Library of Congress

In 1820, a new brick dwelling was built on old foundations of a glebe house which had been built for Fairfax Parish in 1775 and had burned in 1808. A glebe was farm land allocated to a minister to provide part of his compensation. The octagonal wing was probably added before 1860. The Frank Ball family purchased The Glebe in 1920 and lived there until 1983. Developer Preston C. Caruthers subdivided the land but preserved The Glebe House in 1986. Courtesy of the Arlington County Public Library

Artist Augustus Köllner made this wash drawing of Chain Bridge at the Little Falls of the Potomac River on September 30, 1839. At the time there were mills and commercial buildings at the site. Courtesy of the Library of Congress

After serving during the Civil War as the Union Army's first Signal Officer and organizer of the Signal Corps during and after the Civil War, Brig. Gen. Albert J. Myer moved the Signal School to Fort Whipple on Arlington Heights in 1869. Later Myer initiated experiments with various kinds of telephones and field telegraphy and established a network of signal stations at lighthouses and lifesaving stations on the Atlantic coast, leading to a national weather service. When he died in 1880, the name of the army post was changed to Fort Myer in his honor. Courtesy of the National Archives

Fort Myer became the site for some of the army's best training in mounted cavalry drill in the 1890s. This came about partly due to Gen. Philip Sheridan's interest in the development of cavalry tactics and training when he was chief commander of the United States Army. During the Spanish-American War in 1898, Frederic Remington, as well as other artists, visited Fort Myer's great riding hall and captured in drawings the power and concentration of the troopers exercising their mounts in races and jumping. Courtesy of Richard Thompson

The Hume School is believed to have been built in 1891 on land partly donated by Frank Hume and partly purchased by the county from him. The building was made of brick and had two classrooms, one upstairs and one down. It was used for classes until 1956. It became the Arlington Historical Museum operated by the Arlington Historical Society. Watercolor by Wilson Gray, commissioned by the Arlington Trust Company to commemorate the bicentennial of the United States.

The Arlington Experimental Farm was created by an Act of Congress in 1899 on part of the Arlington estate adjacent to Fort Myer, Arlington National Cemetery and Freedmen's Village. Administered by the Department of Agriculture, the farm was used for experimental roads as well as for farming. Shown in the photograph is a road grader at the farm in 1905. In 1940, the Experimental Farm activities were moved to Beltsville, Maryland. Courtesy of the National Archives

A gravity streetcar line using cars and horses similar to the one shown here served the public between Clarendon and the Alexandria County courthouse around 1900. After pulling the car and its passengers up the hill, the horse or mule rode back down the hill on the back of the rail car. Courtesy of the Missouri Historical Society (Railroad #27)

Boating on the Potomac River was a favorite form of recreation about 1910 when this postcard picture was taken. The rebuilt Aqueduct Bridge can be seen in the background with pedestrians and trolley cars crossing. It was replaced by the Francis Scott Key Bridge in 1923. Courtesy of the Virginia Historical Society

The first firehouse was built for the Ballston Volunteer Fire Department, Company 2, organized in 1908, on Ballston Avenue near Fairfax Drive. The first firefighting vehicle was a wagon. The engine shown was a modified Model T Ford truck, purchased later, which carried drums of soda acid and lengths of hose. Courtesy of the Arlington County Fire Department

Before the construction of Jefferson Elementary School, the children from the nearby community attended school at St. John's Church on Columbia Pike. The little girl on the front left of this photograph, taken in 1912 or 1913, was Katherine Mosley (Ross). She became a school teacher and a prominent citizen of the county and the state. Standing behind the children is their teacher, Maria Syphax, the wife of William Syphax, a pioneer in the education of African-American children in the District of Columbia. Courtesy of the Arlington Historical Society

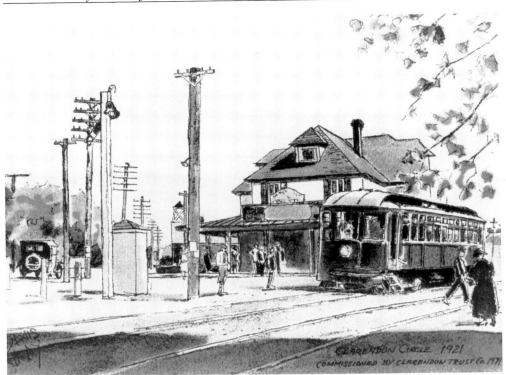

This watercolor of Clarendon Circle as it appeared in 1921 was commissioned by the Clarendon Trust Company in 1971. Behind the streetcar is the building where members of the community gathered to pick up their mail and exchange information. In the center background is the bell tower of the firehouse. The circle was at the intersection of Washington and Wilson boulevards. Courtesy of J. Lawrence Manning

The Francis Scott Key Bridge, named after the author who wrote the text of "The Star Spangled Banner," was completed in 1923. It replaced the old Aqueduct Bridge which is shown just upstream on the Potomac. The old Cherry Smash bottling plant can be seen in the foreground. It was built in 1896, designed by Albert E. Goenner. Photograph taken in 1922, courtesy of the Arlington County Public Library

Sheriff Howard Fields, on the far left, was shown with motorcycle officers Jack Conway, Archie Richardson, Jim East, Hugh Jones, John "Babe" Burke, Roy Cobean and Raymond Crack in 1929 when this photograph was taken in front of the county jail. A separate county police department was established by the county board in 1940 with Harry L. Woodward appointed the first chief of police. Courtesy of the Arlington County Police Department

Near the 14th Street bridges, between the George Washington Memorial Parkway and the Potomac River, a large curling wave with seven seagulls poised in flight above it honors men who go to the sea in ships. The symbolic, bronze-finished cast aluminum sculpture was designed by artist Ernesto Begni Del Piatta in 1930, and placed on its green marble base in 1941 by architect H. W. Corbett. Courtesy of the Arlington County Public Library

Known as the world's biggest office building when it was completed during World War II, the Pentagon contains over 6.5 million square feet of space. At the time of its heaviest use, 37,000 employees worked there. Occupying a 583-acre tract, there are 67 acres of parking space and 30 miles of access roadways. In the center of the building, surrounded by the innermost of five rings, is a five-acre courtyard landscaped like a park with trees and grass, benches and pigeons. Courtesy of the Department of Defense

On September 11, 2001, terrorists hijacked American Airlines Flight 77 out of Dulles International Airport and crashed into the west side of the Pentagon, damaging three of the five rings and killing 189 people. Concerned workers from around the country signed on to the Phoenix Project for rebuilding the Pentagon's damaged area before the one year anniversary of the attack. Photo by Scott Boatright. Courtesy of Fairfax County Fire and Rescue Department

At the beginning of World War II, Fort Myer was used for testing vehicles in open country and rough terrain conditions. In 1941, a new general purpose vehicle designed to replace motorcycles and able to accommodate three men and equipment was tested and found suitable. It was nicknamed "The Jeep" and was adopted by the Army. It proved to be invaluable in service. Courtesy of the Library of Congress

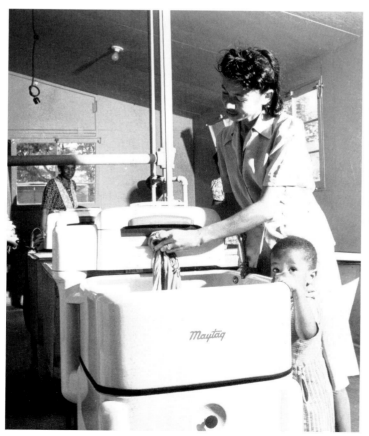

The influx of government workers and the construction of the Pentagon during World War II led to an acute housing shortage in Arlington. One of the ways of solving citizens' needs was the establishment of segregated trailer camps by the Farm Security Administration. This 1942 photograph was taken in the laundry of a community building in one of these camps. Photograph by Marjory Collins. Courtesy of the Library of Congress

Charles Richard Drew was born in 1904 in Washington, D. C. As an African-American physician, he worked both in the chemistry laboratory and in surgery, contributing to science significant discoveries of techniques for the preservation of blood plasma for transfusions and establishment of the American Red Cross blood bank. He and his parents lived on First Street South in Arlington.
Courtesy of the Arlington Historical Society

The construction of the George Washington Memorial Parkway along the steep, rocky Potomac palisades north of Key Bridge was a monumental undertaking. In addition to clearing and leveling the divided four-lane right-of-way, high bridges had to be built over Arlington's stream valleys. The parkway section from Spout Run to Langley was completed by the National Park Service in October 1960. Shown in this 1960 photograph is the parkway's bridge over the Spout Run Valley.
Courtesy of the National Archives

Pierre Charles L'Enfant, of French birth and military training, came to America with General Lafayette and served as an engineer with the American armies during the Revolutionary War. Following the war, he drew up a basic design for Washington City, the design which has influenced the character of the national capital ever since. The outline of this city plan is carved in the top of the monument shown here on the hill near Arlington House. The monument was authorized by Congress and placed in the cemetery when L'Enfant was reburied at Arlington in 1909. Courtesy of the Naval Photographic Center

Wearing uniforms which were designed at the birth of the nation, the ceremonial color guard of the Third Infantry Regiment recalls the heritage of the oldest unit in the United States Army, known as the Old Guard. The unit has served in every major war since 1784. The Old Guard is the Army's official ceremonial unit, which provides around-the-clock guards at the Tomb of the Unknowns at Arlington Cemetery and escorts the President of the United States. It is stationed at Fort Myer, where an Old Guard museum traces the unit's history. Courtesy of the U. S. Army Signal Corps

Many of the Vietnam refugees who came to the Arlington area in the 1970s brought skills, organizational ability and experience needed to help them become a part of the new American community as well as to preserve and express their Vietnamese culture. The Vietnamese Community Center, established in Page Elementary School, was the first of its type in the United States. In the photograph shown here are Truong Cam Khai, a painter, and Hoang Van Chi, an historian. Copyright *Washington Post*; reprinted by permission of the D. C. Public Library

Archie Douglas Syphax and Evelyn Reid Syphax were community-minded residents of Arlington all of their adult lives. They worked tirelessly for improvement of educational, cultural and housing opportunities of many kinds. They were active on boards of directors of many organizations whose goals are to improve living conditions and develop potential talents in individuals who lived and worked in the county. Photo taken in 1988, courtesy of the Syphax family

Elizabeth P. Campbell and Edmund D. Campbell were called the "First Couple of Arlington." Mrs. Campbell was the first woman elected to the Arlington County School Board, led in the integration of Arlington's public schools, and founded public television station WETA in 1961. Mr. Campbell practiced law in the area after 1921 and was known for civil rights work in Norfolk in 1958, and for arguing the "one man, one vote" case before the United States Supreme Court in 1963. He chaired the Arlington County Board twice in the 1940s. *Courtesy of Donald Campbell. Photo by Gerald Martineau.* ©1989 the *Washington Post*. Reprinted with permission.

It was largely due to the microfilming program for Arlington County court records inaugurated in 1977 by Circuit Court Clerk David A. Bell, shown here, that almost all county court records have been retained. An electrical fire in the courthouse on May 20, 1990, burned many files which had been copied on records automated since 1986. In a very few days, necessary records were again available to the courts and the public because of duplicates stored elsewhere. *Courtesy of the Arlington County Circuit Court*

The steeple of Alexandria's City Hall is seen above Gadsby's Tavern, which was photographed from the courtyard in 1936. Photograph by John O. Brostrup, courtesy of The National Archives

X

Alexandria

The flood plain of the Potomac River provided a trading point for the Algonquian tribesmen who welcomed Captain John Smith on his arrival in 1608. In 1654, Margaret Brent patented 700 acres of land in the area where Alexandria would later be founded. That land was purchased in 1669 by John Alexander of Stafford County. In the 1730s, a public warehouse for tobacco inspection was built on the Potomac shore above the mouth of Great Hunting Creek, at the foot of what became Oronoco Street. Legislation passed by the Virginia Assembly in 1749 created the town of Alexandria. The town consisted of sixty acres of land which were laid out in lots and sold at auction. The town included a market place and a public landing.

Commerce came easily to Alexandria because of its location at the fall line of the Potomac, and soon large quantities of products from areas around the town were being shipped to other colonies and foreign ports. Ships coming into port brought a vast variety of products from all over the world.

Shipbuilding yards operated throughout the 19th and into the 20th century. Other industries included the company of Smith and Perkins, which was producing thirty locomotives and three hundred rail cars annually by the mid-1850s. In the 20th century, automobiles and aircraft were produced in the city. Alexandria was the seat of Fairfax County government from 1752 to 1800 when the town officially became part of the District of Columbia.

With the presence of extensive commercial and governmental activities in Alexandria, numerous taverns and shops were established. Among the town's craftsmen were potters, glassmakers and silversmiths. Churches have been vital to the character of the old town. Christ Church was completed in 1773; the Presbyterian Meeting House was in use by 1794. Methodists and Baptists had congregations in Alexandria by 1795 and 1803, respectively. A Catholic chapel was built in 1795, and Beth El, the Reform Jewish Congregation, was formed in the 19th century.

In the French and Indian War, British General Edward Braddock landed his army in Alexandria and made the town the rear base for the war's opening campaign. John Carlyle's house was the site of a grand council in which Braddock and the royal governors of five colonies planned the campaign which ended in disastrous defeat for the army approaching Fort Duquesne. Alexandria did not suffer damage from fighting in the American Revolution, but it was visited by a British man-of-war during the War of 1812, and local militia units at Belvoir mansion were bombarded as the British ship left the area. During the Civil War, Federal troops occupied the town throughout the war and reconstruction.

Through almost all the nineteenth century, Alexandria served as the focal point of Northern Virginia's economy. The area's bankers and leading professional services were located there; and when railroads began to be built in mid-century, Alexandria became their hub and the point where land transport connected with water transport.

From its early history, Alexandria was a town where the education of its children held a place of importance. There were grammar schools for white boys and girls before the end of the 18th century.

Though known for its slave market, Alexandria also was home to a number of free blacks who established communities in the town by 1850. After the Civil War, numerous freed slaves lived in the city. By the end of the century, an annual celebration of the Emancipation Proclamation was held on September 22, bringing large numbers of celebrants by train to Alexandria to hear speakers such as Frederick Douglass and Virginia's African-American congressman and educator, John Mercer Langston.

Through most of its long history, Alexandria has had an outstanding newspaper in the Alexandria *Gazette*, which began in 1785 as the *Virginia Journal and Advertizer*. Samuel Snowden was the editor in 1800. He was followed by his son, Edgar, and his grandson, Edgar, Jr. The paper has been in continuous publication since its founding.

The 20th century movement towards restoration of old buildings was begun in 1903 with the formation of the Society for the Restoration of Historic Alexandria and continued with the Alexandria Association, formed in 1932. In 1946, the city created a large historic district.

Alexandria is one of Virginia's most active tourism destinations, with a busy annual calendar of activities reflecting the colonial traditions and architecture of its historic Old Town section. As it led the state in the preservation of historical and archaeological sites and structures, it now leads in fostering an appreciation of the heritage of history in its ambience.

From a few hundred original settlers in 1749, Alexandria's population grew by 2000 to 128,283.

ON SEPTEMBER 6, 1654, THIS SITE WAS INCLUDED IN A PATENT OF 700 ACRES GRANTED BY THE COLONY OF VIRGINIA TO

MISTRESS MARGARET BRENT
(c1601 — c1671)

AN EXTRAORDINARY WOMAN, SHE SPENT MOST OF HER ADULT LIFE FIGHTING DISCRIMINATION OF HER SEX. SHE WAS THE FIRST PRIVATE OWNER OF THE RECTANGULAR TRACT OF LAND ON THE POTOMAC RIVER ABOVE HUNTING CREEK THAT BECAME THE NUCLEUS OF ALEXANDRIA.

ERECTED BY
THE MOUNT VERNON CHAPTER
DAUGHTERS OF THE AMERICAN REVOLUTION
1978

Erected in 1978 by the Mount Vernon Chapter of The Daughters of the American Revolution, this plaque honors the memory of Margaret Brent, a settler and landowner in Maryland and Virginia in the 17th century. In Maryland, Margaret Brent had been a well-known legal advocate, appearing in court more than a hundred times. She is the first woman on record to ask for voting rights.
Courtesy of the photographer, Richard Netherton

Now the Alexandria Visitors Center, the Ramsay House was the home of William Ramsay, a Scottish merchant who had settled in Dumfries around 1742. He bought several Alexandria town lots at the 1749 sale and placed his house at King and Fairfax streets. Ramsay married Ann McCarty Ball, a cousin of George Washington. Courtesy of the Alexandria Convention & Visitors Association

Designed by architect James Wren, Christ Church was built in 1767-1773 on land donated by John Alexander. Among the worshipers at Christ Church were George Washington and Robert E. Lee. Colonel Lee attended services here in April of 1861, on the day before he went to Richmond, where he eventually rose to command of the Confederate armies. Courtesy of the Alexandria Convention and Visitor's Association

The Old Presbyterian Meeting House was constructed in 1836, replacing an earlier building that was burned. Alexandria's Scottish settlers, including John Carlyle and William Ramsay, began building their first meeting house in 1774. Dr. James Muir, who served here from 1789 to 1820, conducted Alexandria's memorial service following the death of George Washington. Courtesy of the Alexandria Convention & Visitors Association

The Friendship Fire House at 107 S. Alfred Street was constructed in 1855. It houses a company that was established in 1774 and was long associated with George Washington, who bought a fire engine for Alexandria in Philadelphia in 1775. The firehouse is operated as a museum run by the City of Alexandria. From the postcard collection of Tony Chaves

Captains Row, the 100 block of Prince Street in Alexandria, preserves its original cobblestone pavement and the handsome town residences constructed there in the 18th century. The houses on the street have been beautifully restored, thanks in part to the efforts of Gay Montague Moore, an historian and one of the leaders of Alexandria's restoration movement. Courtesy of the Alexandria Convention & Visitors Association

Founded in 1785, the Alexandria Academy was called the Washington School when this photograph was taken sometime before 1916. It included a free school for poor children, endowed by George Washington. The building became the property of the Alexandria School Board in 1884. The old building has been renovated by the Historic Alexandria Foundation under the guidence of Al Cox, A.I.A., and Dr. Peter Smith, Architectural Historian. The grounds have been improved by landscape architect Ron Kagawa. Courtesy of the Library of Congress

Constructed in 1792 by John Wise next door to the older Mason's Ordinary, this hotel was leased in 1796 by John Gadsby. Notables of Alexandria, including George Washington, gathered here on special occasions. The older portion of the tavern was Washington's headquarters when he became colonel of the militia in 1754. It is operated by the City of Alexandria. Courtesy of the Alexandria Convention & Visitors Association

John Gadsby ran the tavern that bears his name from 1796 until 1808. While in Alexandria he was noted for his hospitality, entertaining such notables as George Washington and Thomas Jefferson. Among his progeny were two distinguished artists: his grandson John Gadsby Chapman, born in Alexandria in 1808; and his great-grandson, Conrad Wise Chapman, who was a Confederate soldier and artist during the Civil War. Portrait by John Gadsby Chapman courtesy of Gadsby's Tavern

Built by Robert Young around 1812 for a dwelling, this house became in the 1820s the office of Franklin & Armfield, one of the country's leading slave traders. Pens were built on the grounds adjacent to the house for the confinement of men, women and children who were to be sold. In the 1860s the proprietors were Price and Birch. Courtesy of the Library of Congress

Once a branch of the Alexandria Public Library, Lloyd House is believed to have been constructed in 1797 by taverner John Wise. In 1832, the house was purchased by merchant John Lloyd, whose family owned it until 1918, when it became the home of William Albert Smoot, a businessman and mayor of Alexandria. Courtesy of the Alexandria Public Library

The Stabler-Leadbeater Apothecary operated from 1792 to 1933. When it closed, it contained a large collection of artifacts, records, and medicinal supplies which have been preserved for posterity by the Landmarks Society of Alexandria. Daniel Webster, Henry Clay, John C. Calhoun, Robert E. Lee and Martha Washington shopped here. Photograph by Frederick D. Nichols in 1940, courtesy of the Library of Congress

The Protestant Episcopal Theological Seminary was established in 1823 under the leadership of Bishop Richard Channing Moore. Aspinwall Hall, shown in the photograph, was dedicated in 1859. On the grounds of the seminary is the Episcopal High School, founded in 1839. The grounds of the Episcopal Theological Seminary were landscaped by Andrew Jackson Downing. From the Brady Collection, courtesy of the National Archives

Henry "Light Horse Harry" Lee, the father of Robert E. Lee, was a distinguished leader of the Virginia dragoons during the American Revolution, and later was governor of Virginia. From the eulogy he delivered at the death of George Washington come the words "first in war, first in peace, and first in the hearts of his countrymen." Engraving by J. Herring after a portrait by Gilbert Stuart. Courtesy of the Library of Congress

Built in 1795, this house was acquired a few years later by William Fitzhugh of Chatham, in Stafford County. Fitzhugh's daughter, Mary Lee, was married here to George Washington Parke Custis, the grandson of Martha Washington, in 1804. Henry "Light Horse Harry" Lee, moved here with his wife, Ann Hill Carter, and their five children in 1812. His youngest son was Robert E. Lee, then five years old. Etching courtesy of the artist, Elizabeth Ochs

Benjamin Hallowell was a Quaker schoolmaster who moved to Alexandria and started a school for boys at 609 Oronoco Street in 1824. Hallowell moved his school to Lloyd House on Washington Street in 1825, moving again to a sugar refinery and tobacco warehouse adjacent to the Lloyd House. Hallowell was a major figure in the establishment of Alexandria's Lyceum and the town's waterworks. Courtesy of the Alexandria Library

The Lyceum was named for a c. 335 B.C. school led by the philosopher Aristotle. In Alexandria, Benjamin Hallowell was elected president of the organization and gave its first lecture when the building opened in 1839. Such national figures as John Quincy Adams and Caleb Cushing were among the lecturers. After many years of use for other purposes, the Lyceum became the city's history museum and lecture hall. Courtesy of the Lyceum

Constructed in 1851-52 for the Bank of the Old Dominion, the Atheneum is shown in a photograph from the Mathew Brady Collection as it appeared in 1864, when it was a commissary for the Union Army. It was acquired by the Northern Virginia Fine Arts Association, and used to exhibit art and to hold lectures. Courtesy of the National Archives

A view of Alexandria's riverfront from Pioneer Mill, which was located at the foot of Duke Street, shows a variety of vessels and warehouses. The Pioneer Mill was built in 1853-54. During the Civil War milling operations ceased. The mill burned in 1899. Courtesy of the Alexandria Public Library

Built in 1856 by a Lighthouse Board under the United States Department of the Treasury, the Jones Point Lighthouse ceased to function in 1926. Through the efforts of Alexandria residents led by Leona Kemper and the Mount Vernon Chapter of the Daughters of the American Revolution, the lighthouse was restored and the light was again illuminated on October 29, 1993. The building is on the site of the first cornerstone of the District of Columbia, placed there on April 15, 1791. Courtesy of the photographer, Richard Netherton

Dedicated in 1887, John A. Elder's statue of "Appomattox" faces south from its pedestal at the busy intersection of Prince and South Washington streets. At this location, Alexandria's Confederate volunteers were mustered on May 24, 1861. The figure represents a Confederate soldier viewing the battlefields after Gen. Robert E. Lee's surrender to Gen. Ullyses S. Grant at Appomattox on April 9, 1865. Courtesy of the photographer, Richard Netherton

Concerned about the lack of hospital facilities in the community, Juliana Johns, daughter of the city's Episcopal bishop, Dr. John Johns, called a meeting in 1872 of her "charitably disposed" friends to consider "the formation of a society to establish and control a hospital." The first facility was opened in 1873 on the southwest corner of Duke and South Fairfax streets. Courtesy of Alexandria Hospital

Robb Kidd was a carrying-in-boy who worked in a glass factory in Alexandria. He alternated working the day shift every other week. The photograph was taken in June of 1911 by Lewis Hine, who took photographs of working children for the National Child Labor Committee, which was attempting to abolish child labor. Courtesy of the National Archives

Mr. Madella's class at the Snowden School for Negro Boys posed for this photograph about 1913. George L. Seaton contracted to build Snowden in 1867 for Alexandria's African American boys, for whom there was no public school education prior to the Civil War. Courtesy of the Black History Resource Center, and photographer Richard Netherton

The fourth grade class of Hallowell's School for Girls is seen in front of the school c. 1913-1915. Hallowell School was on Alfred Street, and was built in 1867 by master carpenter George L. Seaton. It was in use until the Parker-Gray School opened on Wythe Street in 1920. Courtesy of the Black History Resource Center and photographer Richard Netherton

Standing in front of the 1803 Alfred Street Baptist Church are Mrs. Annie B. Rose, left, and Mrs. Lorraine Funn Atkins. Mrs. Rose was the daughter of a former slave, Lewis H. Bailey, who was once sold in the Alexandria slave market. She is remembered for her tireless work on behalf of the poor and elderly citizens of Alexandria. Mrs. Rose joined Mrs. Atkins in her successful fight against demolition of the church in the 1970s, leading to the creation of the Alexandria Society for the Preservation of Black Heritage. Courtesy of the Black History Resource Center

The Torpedo Factory was completed in 1920 and produced torpedoes for peace-time use between the two World Wars and for wartime use in the 1940s. In 1969 the complex was purchased by the City of Alexandria, which established an Art Center in two of the buildings in 1974, at the instigation of Marian Van Landingham, the center's first director. The Torpedo Factory Art Center houses the City's Archeology Museum and Research Laboratory and studios for 155 or more artists. Courtesy of the Torpedo Factory

Located on Shuter's Hill, the George Washington Masonic National Memorial dominates the skyline in Alexandria. Begun in 1923, the building's principal architects were Helmle & Corbett of New York. Carl R. Parker of Olmsted Brothers was landscape architect. The building's primary purpose was to house the relics of George Washington, first master of Alexandria-Washington Lodge No. 22. Courtesy of the Arlington County Library

Elizabeth-Anne Campbell Campagna was from 1961 to 1985 Executive Director of the Alexandria Community Y, which was renamed the Campagna Center in her honor after the Alexandria facility broke from the national YWCA in 1974. In 1995, the Campagna Center celebrated 50 years of service to Alexandria. Courtesy of the Campagna Center

Following the last run of the Southern Crescent *on February 1, 1979, the crew posed in front of the engine of Southern Railway's last overnight luxury train, which was being taken over by Amtrak. From left to right are flagman Robert C. Fields, conductor M. E. Robertson, Jr., engineer Clifton W. Mattox and fireman E. T. Steele. The last run of the* Crescent *ended Southern's passenger service from Washington to New Orleans, begun in the early 1900s. Mattox, Fields, and Robertson were from Alexandria.* Courtesy of the photographer, Warren Mattox, son of C. W. Mattox.

Photographed before a portrait of Robert E. Lee on his horse, Traveller, Richard Bales is seen examining a volume of Civil War songs. The Alexandria-born composer and conductor wrote the suites Union *and* Confederacy *from marches, ballads, and love songs of the Civil War. He also arranged a suite of Revolutionary War music. Bales was conductor of the National Gallery Orchestra from 1943 to 1985.* Courtesy of the Alexandria Library

Winslow Homer's painting entitled "Home, Sweet Home" was first exhibited in April 1863 when the mood of both sides was changing from energy and enthusiasm to weariness and thoughts of home. The soldiers here listen in thoughtful silence to the military band playing for their comrades at ease on the ground, and well within earshot of the hostile troops whose tents are pitched across the river. In this Homer also reflected the mood throughout the home front in Northern Virginia. "Home, Sweet Home" established Homer in the ranks of leading American artists of his time. Courtesy National Gallery of Art

XI

The War That No One Wanted

The Civil War came to Virginia too swiftly for Virginians to become united in heart and mind before they were committed to the terrible struggle. Virginia voted for the Constitutional Union candidate in the election of 1860, and joined with other moderates in the upper South to keep Virginia in the Union during the early months of 1861. Only when hostilities began at Fort Sumter and Lincoln called for troops to maintain the Union did state loyalty prevail and end the chance of conciliation. Virginia's Ordinance of Secession was passed on April 17, 1861, and was ratified by popular vote on May 23rd. Union troops entered Northern Virginia on May 24th.

In Northern Virginia there were misgivings about secession and pockets of Unionists remained alongside pockets of Secessionists throughout the war that neither wanted. Initially, many Northern Virginians chose to leave their land and go to areas north or south where their personal sentiments were welcome and where they could stay with friends or relatives. The best-known instance of this may possibly have been Wilmer McLean, who moved from Manassas, where his home was on the battlefield of July 1861, and relocated his home to Appomattox to "secure relief from visitation of an army." The McLean house at Appomattox Court House was the scene of Lee's surrender to Grant in 1865.

The important role that the land between the Rappahannock and the Potomac would play in the war evolved more slowly. The first major encounter of the war at Manassas in July 1861 allowed the Confederates to move up to the edge of the Union Army's ring of forts around Washington where they remained throughout the summer and fall of 1861. Federal troops tried to outflank this line by crossing the Potomac River and seizing Leesburg in Loudoun County but were turned back disastrously at Ball's Bluff in October 1861. At the same time, Confederate batteries downriver virtually blockaded Washington city by closing the Potomac channel to shipping during the winter of 1861-62. From the autumn of 1861 onward, the area's role in the war gradually took on its shape. Viewed from the North it became the site of the fortifications protecting the city of Washington, the port of Alexandria, the navigable channel of the Potomac, and the landing at Aquia Creek. On the region's southern edge along the Rappahannock, Fredericksburg became the gateway to the road south; and at its western end Warrenton, Aldie and Leesburg were posted on the routes to the Shenandoah Valley. Thus it developed into the vital staging area for Union armies campaigning to the south—a place of depots and warehouses, stockpiling all sorts of military supplies and equipment, and a transportation and communication corridor to assure timely delivery of supplies and reinforcements to Union armies in the field.

Viewed from the South, these depots became tempting targets of opportunity. Equipment and supplies captured there and sent South were invaluable to the Confederate armies whose regular sources of supply were shut off by the Union blockade. And Union troops who were retained in Northern Virginia to protect the national capital or to guard its lines of transport and communication were not able to join the Army of the Potomac in the battlefields around Richmond. The importance of Fauquier and Loudoun counties as eastern gateways to the lower Shenandoah Valley and Maryland was also of paramount importance in Confederate strategic planning. In 1862 Lee led his Army of Northern Virginia into Maryland (Antietam) by way of the fords in Loudoun County's Potomac River boundary. And in 1864 Jubal Early's corps returned to Virginia by this route after it had reached the outskirts of Washington in a desperate drive through Maryland. Maneuvering through the passes in the Blue Ridge Mountains, Stonewall Jackson made Fauquier,

Loudoun and Prince William counties the scene of his brilliant campaigns in and out of the Valley; and later John Singleton Mosby made these areas part of his "Confederacy." It was pivotal ground for both sides.

The soldiers' war was not the only one waged in Northern Virginia. Day in and day out other wars were being fought here and were producing their share of casualties and heros.

The home front was the scene of one of these other wars. As civilian travel was suppressed by both Northern and Southern occupiers, the isolation of farm families deepened and normal civilian commerce all but ceased. Farming was carried on by women, children, slaves and old men. Simple survival became its objective, and even the meager yields of these efforts were constantly subject to seizure by foragers, stragglers and vandals. Women who stayed on their land to keep it from being vandalized and to keep their families together displayed resilience and determination which matched the courage of the battlefield. Food, clothing, fabric, soap, paper, metal products of all kinds, and medicine were beyond the reach of all but a very few on the Virginia home front. Writing in the summer of 1863, a Fauquier County woman observed:

> From having a comfortable table, I am reduced to a bacon bone. The Yankeys have overrun my garden and injured what they did not take away. . . . I have a very sick grandchild and several servants sick with no suitable medicine. May God give me grace and strength to bear my burden knowing that. (Robertson, *Civil War Virginia,* 108.)

Fighting and the rigors of occupation took a severe toll on the home front in Virginia, but collapse of the Confederate internal economy had an equally deadly effect as inflation rose. Under these pressures civilian morale deteriorated and law and order disappeared in many areas of Virginia where normal civil government ceased to exist.

Going on through the military lines and throughout the home front another war was fought. This was the secret war of smuggling, spying, clandestine travel and black market commerce. An efficient Confederate network existed for passing information and people through Northern Virginia. Newspapers from major east coast Northern cities were available in Richmond a day after they were printed. High value and easily transported goods such as medicines and machine tools were favored in this clandestine traffic. But it is said that once an entire locomotive was brought from the North one piece at a time to be reassembled on Confederate tracks. While this traffic persisted throughout the war, however, it never reached a level that eased the war's impact on the home front.

Still another war carried on across Northern Virginia took place in workshops and factories. The mobilization of Northern industry and technology was a major achievement, and no scene is more convincing evidence of this than Mathew Brady's photographs of timber, steel rails, prefabricated bridge components and other military materiel stockpiled in the Alexandria railroad yards. Much of this materiel found its way into the military railroads, workshops and warehouses of the Union armies in Northern Virginia in efforts to keep this area functioning as the sword, shield and arsenal of the Union capital.

The chief economic legacy of the war was the devastation it brought to the area's natural resources. The cultivated farmland, the water resources and natural habitats, and, perhaps most of all, the area's hardwood forests all were treated as expendable by the armies of both sides as they campaigned, built fortifications, foraged for food and fodder, and wasted what they could not use. Expenditure of the area's natural resources in this way would affect the environment and economy of Northern Virginia for a century afterward.

The Civil War in Northern Virginia may be viewed here from the perspectives of these activities, all of which went on together during the years of conflict, and some of which lasted long after the fighting ceased.

Before dawn on the morning of May 24, 1861, Federal troops from New York crossed the Long Bridge (site of the present Fourteenth Street Bridge) and the Aqueduct Bridge (site of present Key Bridge) from Washington and Georgetown into Virginia. At the same time the gunboat USS Pawnee *landed a detachment on the Alexandria waterfront. Winslow Homer sketched the scene at the Long Bridge, shown here, for publication later in* Harper's Weekly *magazine. On the Virginia shore, the Federal troops fortified the approaches to the Potomac bridges and sent scouting patrols in the direction of Ball's Crossroads and Falls Church to watch for activity by Confederate units forming in Virginia.* Courtesy of the National Park Service

Immediately following secession, Virginia designated military districts and began organizing volunteer units. Recruiting began in a wave of patriotic excitement stirred by the firing on Fort Sumter, and it rose rapidly as President Lincoln declared a blockade of Southern ports and then sent Federal troops into Northern Virginia. Expecting a short and glorious fight, young men in Virginia enthusiastically filled the ranks of state and local militia units, which were then consolidated into larger regiments established by the new Confederate States' War Department. The drawing shown here depicts a high-spirited Confederate recruiting rally at Woodstock in Shenandoah County in the spring of 1861. Source: Willey and Millhollen, *Embattled Confederates*

As hastily-mobilized Federal troops crossed the Potomac and cautiously moved out into Fairfax County, they encountered scouts from hastily-recruited Confederate units assembling near Manassas in Prince William County. Typical of the scenes in this opening phase of the hostilities is this Harper's Weekly *engraving of Confederate scouts seen by Federal pickets in the vicinity of the village of Falls Church.* Courtesy of *Harper's Pictorial War Record*

By June 1861 both Union and Confederate units were active around Washington. On one occasion Federal troops were sent out by train to positions guarding the railroad then running between Alexandria and Leesburg. A Confederate scouting force near the village of Vienna swept the train with shot and brought it to a stop. Following a skirmish, the Confederates retired to Fairfax Court House and the train hastily returned to Alexandria, leaving its passengers to make their way back as well as they could. It was history's first reported use of a railroad in military combat operations. Courtesy of the National Archives

As soon as Union troops entered Virginia, the Arlington Heights, the Potomac bridges, and the town of Alexandria were fortified. But Congress, convinced that secession would be brief, initially resisted proposals to build more extensive fortifications. This changed after the First Battle of Manassas in July 1861, and gradually a series of 23 semi-permanent earthen forts and redoubts were constructed to protect the approaches to Washington and Alexandria from Northern Virginia. The circle around Washington was closed by constructing 12 similar forts on the Maryland side. These fortifications, plus the location of numerous battery positions, eventually numbering some 70 major earthworks, military roads and railroads are shown in the map prepared in 1865 by the War Department's topographical engineers. Courtesy of the National Archives

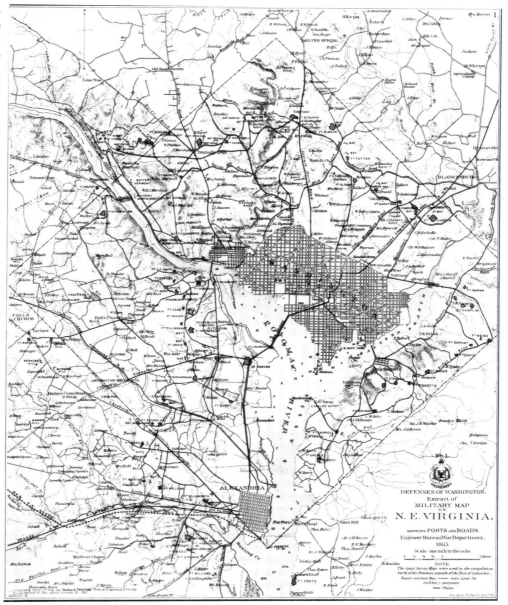

While newly-formed regiments from the Northern states arrived by train in response to President Lincoln's call for volunteers, newly-formed Confederate units gathered near Manassas under the command of General P.G.T. Beauregard and in the Shenandoah Valley under the command of General Joseph Johnston. Many of the recruits and much of the equipment for these armies moved at the speed that a man could march or a mule team could walk. The drawing by a Confederate soldier, shown here, depicts heavy-looking field artillery being hauled by teams of six oxen. The sketch is labeled "A Confederate Bull Battery previous to the Battle of Bull Run." Courtesy of the Fairfax County Public Library Photographic Archive

As the Federal troops began to extend their network of forts and fortified crossroads, Upton's Hill, near Falls Church, was particularly important. In the summer of 1861, Union troops, mainly from New York, fortified this hill with earthworks called Fort Ramsay and built an observation and signal tower. The sketch shown here was made in October 1861 by Arthur Lumley, whose pictures were published in the Illustrated London News. Courtesy of the Northern Virginia Regional Park Authority

In the summer and fall of 1861 Confederate efforts to stop Potomac River traffic effectively blockaded the city of Washington. One of the most important Confederate shore batteries was at Evansport (now Quantico). The fortifications shown in this Harper's Weekly engraving were sketched by an officer of a Union patrol flotilla in November 1861.

In March 1862 Federal forces moved to clear out all Confederate shore batteries between Washington and the Chesapeake Bay. The Confederate blockade of Washington thus was ended and Union forces occupied Aquia Creek to rebuild it and use it as a supply depot for the Army of the Potomac.

The fortifications around Washington City were maintained and expanded throughout the war, and a field army of substantial size was retained in Northern Virginia to prevent Confederate forces from threatening the Union capital. Photographs of the camps, such as that of a New York regiment shown here overlooking Alexandria, give the impression of being decorated for a special ceremonial event, but the rows of decorative trees and topiary arches were everyday amenities invented by the troops themselves.

Photo from the Brady Collection

During the winter of 1861-62 Confederate forces in Northern Virginia concentrated around Centreville. In the spring of 1862 Confederate General Joseph Johnston moved his forces to the Rappahannock for a better position to protect the Confederate capital. As they evacuated the rail center at Manassas Junction, the Confederates removed what they could and destroyed what was left. The engraving here from the Illustrated London News *shows Union cavalry scouts entering the desolated junction in March 1862.*

Courtesy of the Library of Virginia

In November 1861, the Union's new Army of the Potomac held a Grand Review. In the fields between Munson's Hill and Bailey's Crossroads in Fairfax County, approximately 100,000 men passed in review for President Abraham Lincoln and other distinguished Federal officials. Courtesy of the Library of Virginia

Following the First Battle of Manassas, Confederate General Beauregard made his headquarters at Fairfax Court House, where, in October 1861, a conference was held with President Jefferson Davis to consider an early attack on Washington. Davis, however, wary of sentiment in the Confederate Congress and among some state governors, did not approve any plan to invade the Federal City. As a result, Confederate forces retired to Centreville for the winter. This photograph of the Fairfax courthouse building shows Union troops who quickly moved into the former Confederate outpost when it was evacuated. T. H. O'Sullivan photo, courtesy of the Library of Congress

In the winter of 1861-62, the Confederate forces at Centreville built extensive earthworks to protect against the new Army of the Potomac. A military railroad connected Centreville with the Orange and Alexandria Railroad at Manassas Junction. When the forts were abandoned by the Confederates in April 1862, the Union troops found that painted logs had been placed in many of in the gun ports to deceive observers and make it appear that the forts were heavily armed. These so-called "Quaker Guns" were photographed by Mathew Brady as the Union army reoccupied Centreville. Courtesy of the Library of Congress

In 1862, General John Pope was appointed leader of a new Union army, called the Army of Virginia, with orders to march on the Confederate capital down the railway tracks of the Orange & Alexandria Railroad. This move was thwarted by General Robert E. Lee, who brought troops from the defenses of Richmond up to the vicinity of Manassas where, in August 1862, the Union Army was soundly defeated in the Second Battle of Manassas. The engraving from Harper's Weekly *here shows an incident in the battle where a Confederate unit, having run out of ammunition, carried on by throwing rocks at the advancing Federal troops.* Courtesy of the National Archives

Following the defeat of the Union army in the Second Battle of Manassas, the Federal retreat went on until it reached Chantilly (Ox Hill) in Fairfax County. There the Union army's rear guard fought the Confederates to a standstill in the driving rain of a summer thunderstorm. Thereafter Lee abandoned efforts to threaten the Union capital directly and turned his attention to an invasion of Maryland. Courtesy of the Library of Virginia

Loudoun County's strategic importance to both sides was its position as a gateway from Northern Virginia into Maryland and Pennsylvania. Along the county's 40-mile Potomac boundary were White's Ferry, the ford at Point of Rocks, and the bridge at Harper's Ferry.

The drawing shown here was sketched by the artist Alfred Waud in September 1862 as he watched Lee's Army of Northern Virginia cross the Potomac at White's Ferry in the moonlight on its way to Antietam. Courtesy of the Library of Congress

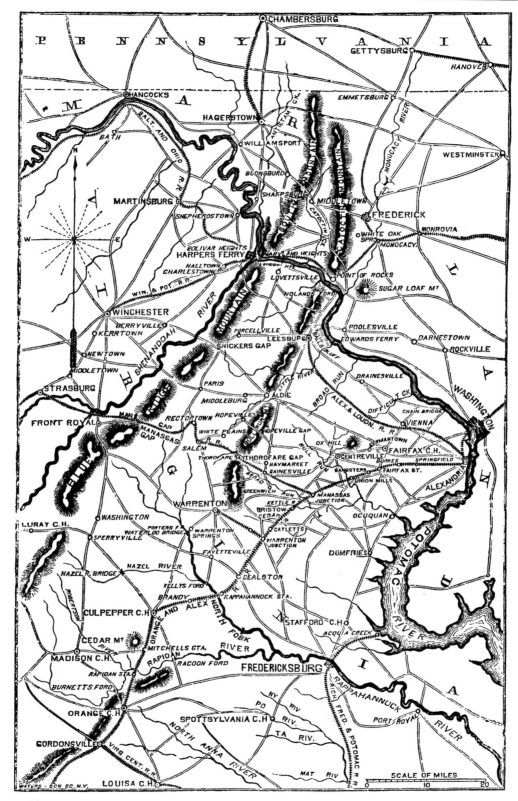

The American Civil War was reported more thoroughly than any war had been up to that time. Places previously unknown except to their residents and neighbors suddenly commanded world attention, resulting in the widespread use of simple maps, easily read and quickly produced, highlighting the information needed to follow the action of the time. The map shown here, covering the area of the campaigns in Northern Virginia, was published in 1866 in Harper's History of the Great Rebellion.

Northern Virginia residents suffered acutely from the constant interference with their freedom to move around their neighborhoods. Throughout the war patrols of Union army units and Confederate guerrilla bands crisscrossed the region and maintained checkpoints on roads and bridges. An artist for Harper's Weekly *sketched the scene shown here, which he described as "secession soldiers preventing Virginia farmers taking supplies over the Long Bridge to Washington."* Sketch courtesy of the Arlington Historical Society.

Military control of travel on the roads in occupied territory was strict and passes were issued to take local residents through the picket posts. The typical pass shown here was valid for the month of December 1864 and authorized William Dyer, a farmer in the vicinity of Ball's Crossroads, to travel with his team of horses to and from the city of Washington. Courtesy of John Gott

As the war strained the fabric of society and the sinews of the economy in both the North and the South, acknowledgment of the support given by women to both the home front and the fighting front increased. Instances of women working in munitions factories or managing farms and businesses were justifiably singled out for praise. Many more women supported the armies by sewing and knitting, cooking, washing clothes, assisting convalescents, comforting the dying, and doing hundreds of other dull but needed services. Source: *Harper's Weekly*

Hardship was often severe for women and families in occupied areas regardless of whether they had Union or Confederate sympathies. Lack of labor, money, horses and mules, seeds and farm implements, plus the inability to travel even short distances, left many women destitute and dependent on Federal military supplies during the winter months. The sketch here depicts a group going to the Union army's commissary for rations near Rappahannock Station, Virginia. It was drawn by the artist Edwin Forbes in February 1864. Courtesy of the Library of Congress

As the war went on, all aspects of Northern Virginia's pre-war economy and society were replaced by a struggle for civilians to survive. Nowhere was this more striking than in the case of blacks who wandered through the area seeking refuge behind the Union army's lines. When the Emancipation Proclamation declared that all slaves who escaped into Union-occupied territory would be considered free, hundreds who had nothing to hold them on the lands of their owners took to the roads on foot as refugees. This drawing shows a family group that was fortunate enough to find a wagon and animals to draw it. Courtesy of the Library of Virginia

Secession sympathizers living in Northern Virginia often assisted Confederate forces by secretly reporting on the activities of Union troops in their vicinity and giving food and shelter to Confederate stragglers and guerrilla bands. Antonia Ford, a 19-year-old girl of Fairfax Court House became so well-known for supplying information to General J.E.B. Stuart that the Confederate cavalry commander made her an honorary aide-de-camp. Antonia Ford was imprisoned for a time because of her activities. Eventually she married a Union army officer whom she met during her detention. Caricature from Harper's Weekly. Courtesy of the Library of Virginia

The Union army tried to suppress Confederate intelligence activities and guerrilla operations by watching and searching homes of secession sympathizers who were suspected of providing "safe houses" to shelter Confederate soldiers or other fugitives being smuggled into or out of Virginia. Prince George's County in Maryland was the eastern center of Confederate espionage, and it produced a steady traffic across the Potomac to the many inlets between the Occoquan River and Aquia Creek on the Virginia shore. Union patrols in this engraving which appeared in Harper's Weekly *early in the war are shown discovering firearms hidden in the furniture.* Courtesy of the Library of Congress

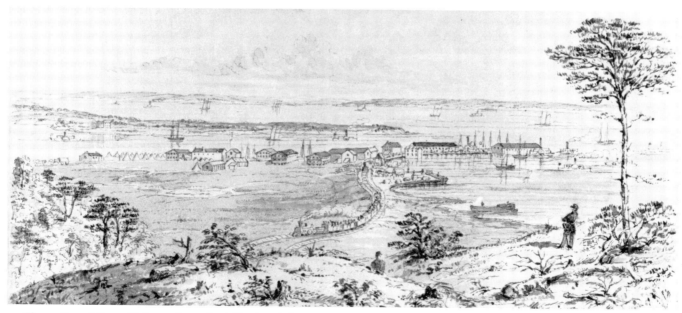

The railroad from Richmond reached Fredericksburg in 1837 and five years later it was extended to the Potomac River at Aquia Creek. Aquia Creek was occupied by Union forces in the spring of 1862, and thereafter it was expanded steadily to become the main depot for supplying the Army of the Potomac in the field and evacuating casualties. The scene shown here was sketched by a Union soldier on the site. Courtesy of Lewis Leigh, Jr.

Northern Virginia could not provide enough food for all the soldiers campaigning there, so beef cattle often were brought from distant sources. Shown here is a rare eyewitness sketch of cattle being swum across the Occoquan River on their way to troops in Fairfax County. Courtesy of the Library of Virginia

It was possible through most of the war for B&O trains to go through Washington, across the Potomac to Alexandria, and onto the tracks of the Orange & Alexandria Railroad to central Virginia or the Alexandria, Loudoun & Hampshire Railroad going west to Leesburg in Loudoun County. Also, at Manassas Junction, the Manassas Gap Railroad branched off to connect with Strasburg in the Shenandoah Valley. The engraving from Harper's Weekly *shown here depicts Union troop trains passing through Thoroughfare Gap in 1864.* Courtesy of the Library of Virginia

The critical importance of railroads in moving troops and the supplies and equipment caused each side to try to deny use of the railroads to the other. The Federal government concentrated its railroad resources under the control of the United States Military Railroad Commission. In the South, utilization of the existing railroad system was seriously hampered because the Confederate government chose not to give their needs the priority required. Thus the main lines in the South were kept operating only by dismantling the lines of minor importance and using their equipment to repair the major lines. Courtesy of the National Archives

When the U. S. Military Railroads Commission took over Alexandria's railroad yard, it became a major center for repairing, servicing and building railroad equipment for the Union Army. Here, also, were stockpiled the rails, lumber, and other equipment and supplies needed for the Military Railroad's Construction Corps and living quarters for many of the "contrabands" and free blacks hired for the work crews. Organized initially in 1862 the Construction Corps repaired and replaced tracks, built bridges, wharves, warehouses, engine houses, and all types of buildings. Shown here is the multi-stalled roundhouse of the O&A Railroad, with a turntable in its center. Courtesy of the Brady Collection, National Archives

Alexandria became one of the most active and crowded waterfronts in the war's theater of operations, with wharves capable of loading 40 vessels at the same time. A huge coal depot at the south end of the Alexandria-Georgetown canal stockpiled fuel for distribution to ships stationed down-river and to advance bases for both army and navy operations farther down the Potomac. Shown here is the last lock in the Alexandria-Georgetown Canal and a military pier for loading river vessels. Courtesy of the Brady Collection, National Archives

Railroad bridges in occupied Northern Virginia were particularly vulnerable to destruction. As a result, the U. S. Military Railroad Commission had to become skilled and efficient in repairing and replacing bridges as fast as they were damaged. An example of these achievements is seen in this photograph of a railroad bridge over Potomac Creek in Stafford County which was reported to have been constructed by Federal soldiers from standing timber in nine days. It was called by President Lincoln the bridge made of "beanpoles and cornstalks." Source: *Northern Virginia Heritage*

The Civil War was the first in which the electric telegraph played a major role. The Federal forces constructed 15,000 miles of wire in the various theaters of the war, while the Confederate armies operated a total of about 1,000 miles of wire. It is estimated that the Union armies' telegraph system handled more than 6.5 million messages during the war. Federal military telegraph lines are shown here in a photograph by Alexander Gardner in April 1864. Courtesy of the National Archives

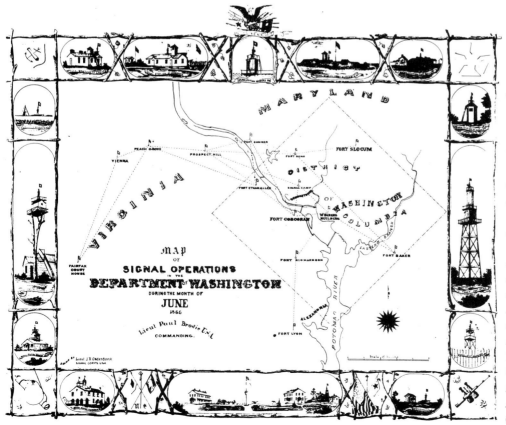

A system of signal stations at key locations served both as an early warning system and a means of coordinating defensive operations if hostile forces approached the capital. From towers, the roofs of buildings, and natural landmarks, signalmen talked to each other by a wig-wag code for signal flags in daylight hours and torches at night. Shown here is a map of the main signal stations in Fairfax County and Washington at the close of hostilities in 1865.

The stations depicted in the border of the map are (clockwise starting with the top row): Fort Lyon; Fort Corcoran; Winder Building (War Department); Fort Slocum; Fort Baker; Fort Sumner; Fort Reno; Peach Orchard (at Tyson's Corner); Vienna; Camp Georgetown; Fairfax Court House; Prospect Hill; Fort Ethan Allen; and Fort Richardson. Courtesy of the National Archives

In November 1862, General Ambrose Burnside moved the Union Army of the Potomac against Fredericksburg where Lee's Army of Northern Virginia occupied a series of hills south of the city. The Union troops crossed the river and occupied the city, but wore themselves out in futile attempts to dislodge the Confederates. Arthur Lumley, a journalist-artist traveling with the Union army, sketched a Federal unit on its way to assault the heights outside the city. The damage to buildings and to personal property emphasize the incalculable cost of the war to those places that felt it first-hand. Courtesy of the Library of Congress

For the first year of the war, Fauquier County was securely in Confederate hands, with their troops stationed at Manassas Junction, Thoroughfare Gap and in the Blue Ridge. But after the Second Battle of Manassas, Union troops occupied key places in the county from the fall of 1862 to the end of the war. The engraving from Harper's Weekly shown here depicts a scene at Warrenton's historic Warren Green Hotel as Union General McClellan said good-by to his officers after he was relieved from command of the Army of the Potomac in November 1862. Courtesy of the Fauquier *Times-Democrat*

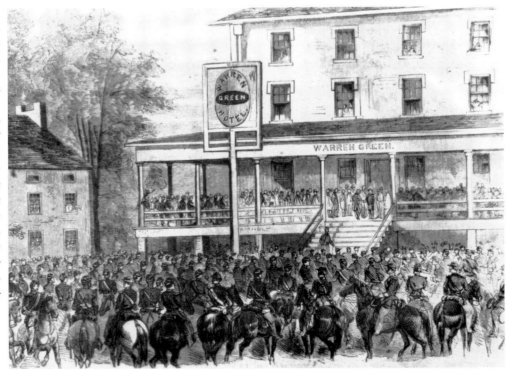

Loudoun County's roads and river crossings attained an almost unique strategic value as gateways to Maryland and to the Shenandoah Valley. Anyone going to or from the Valley had to go through Key's (Vestal's) Gap, Ashby's Gap, or Snicker's Gap. Similarly, anyone going into Maryland could easily cross at one of Loudoun County's bridges or fords, such as White's Ferry, Point of Rocks, Edwards' Ferry and Harper's Ferry. The engraving from Harper's Weekly *shown here depicts the "Leesburg Bridge" across the Potomac about 13 miles below Harper's Ferry as it appeared in June 1861 when it was held by Confederate troops.*

The painting by Armand Dumaresq, called "Mosby's Return From the Greenback Raid," shows the partisan leader with his followers and prisoners returning to their home base after wrecking a train on the Baltimore & Ohio Railroad line near Harper's Ferry in October 1864. Mosby made off with a large quantity of U.S. currency being shipped by train from the Union army's paymaster. Reports of the exploit in both Northern and Southern newspapers romanticized the raid and inspired the interpretation given to it in Dumaresq's painting. Courtesy of the Museum of the Confederacy

On the night of March 9-10, 1863, Union General Edwin Stoughton was asleep in his headquarters in the home of Dr. William Gunnell, in Fairfax Court House, when he was jolted awake by a slap on his bare bottom and informed that he had been captured by Mosby. Moments later the general, two captains, 30 other soldiers and 58 horses were rounded up and taken through Fairfax Station and Centreville to Warrenton as prisoners of war. Next morning when President Lincoln learned of the incident, he observed that he would have no trouble making another general, but he sincerely regretted losing the horses. The Gunnell house where Stoughton's capture occurred still stands in the city of Fairfax. Courtesy of the Fairfax County Public Library Photographic Archive

One of Mosby's notable raids resulted in the destruction at Berryville of a 525-wagon train of military supplies going from Harper's Ferry to General Sheridan's Union army in Winchester in August 1864. Mosby's battalion, armed with a cannon, caught the convoy during a rest period and spread havoc among both the wagon train and its escort. Mosby's men captured, plundered and burned the wagons. They left the scene with more than 300 prisoners, 700 horses and mules, over 200 beef cattle, and valuable military supplies. The scene shown here was published in Harper's Weekly. Courtesy of the Library of Virginia

After surrender of the Army of Northern Virginia on April 9, 1865, Union army headquarters issued a warning that unless Mosby voluntarily surrendered, Federal forces would be sent to round up his men. On April 21, 1865, Mosby summoned his men to meet in a field near the present town of Marshall in Fauquier County. Here, with 200 of his rangers assembled, Mosby formally disbanded the 43d Battalion of Virginia Cavalry in preference to surrendering it. Mosby's men disappeared into the crowds of Confederate veterans making their way back to their homes. General Grant awarded Mosby a parole on the same terms given to General Lee's other officers. Courtesy of the Fauquier Heritage Society

Much of the Northern Virginia slave population drifted into areas occupied by Union army garrisons. The Federal government in 1863 established several special villages for refugees, the largest and longest-lasting of which was Freedmen's Village, located on the site of present Arlington National Cemetery and Henderson Hall. The villages provided food, clothing, shelter, medical care, schools, and training in employable skills. A hospital and home for disabled and elderly residents were built. Freedmen's Village, depicted in the sketch shown here, continued under supervision of the War Department until it was closed in 1888. Courtesy of the Library of Virginia

The forested areas of Arlington, Fairfax and Prince William counties were systematically cut down by the occupying armies to provide wood for fortifications, buildings of all types, bridges, fuel, and even corduroy roads. A New York soldier wrote: "I remember to have watched from our encampment the disappearance of these forests, and as giant after giant was seen to fall along the edge of the woods, the forest seemed to melt away and disappear as snow gradually dissolves from the hillsides in the springtime." The war all but wiped out Northern Virginia's hardwood forests. Courtesy of the National Park Service

The notorious Union Loyalty Oath was used throughout the war and reconstruction. The copy of that oath shown here was executed in 1869 by one George Hawxhurst of Fairfax County who adopted the privilege of Quakers to "affirm" rather than "swear to" the statement he made. Courtesy of the Fairfax County Circuit Court Archives

OATH PRESCRIBED BY ACT OF JULY 2, 1862.

[This oath must be taken and subscribed by every person elected or appointed to office in any of the five Military Districts, before a notary public or some magistrate authorized by law to administer oaths, before entering upon the duties of his Office. (See Section 9, Act of July 19, 1867.) The signature of the notary public or magistrate should be attested by the signature of a clerk of a court of record, under the seal of the court.]

I, *Geo. W. Hawxhurst* of *Fairfax C. H.* county of *Fairfax*, and State of *Virginia*, do solemnly *affirm* that I have never voluntarily borne arms against the United States since I have been a citizen thereof; that I have voluntarily given no aid, countenance, counsel, or encouragement to persons engaged in armed hostility thereto; that I have neither sought, nor accepted, nor attempted to exercise the functions of any office whatever, under any authority, or pretended authority, in hostility to the United states; that I have not yielded a voluntary support to any pretended government, authority, power, or constitution, within the United States hostile or inimical thereto. And I do further *affirm* that, to the best of my knowledge and ability, I will support and defend the Constitution of the United States against all enemies, foreign and domestic; that I will bear true faith and allegiance to the same; that I take this obligation freely, without any mental reservation or purpose of evasion; and that I will well and faithfully discharge the duties of the office on which I am about to enter: so help me God.

Geo. W. Hawxhurst

Affirmed and subscribed before me, this *6* day of *Sept* A. D. 186*9*.

XII

People and Places Throughout the Centuries

The waterfall at Great Falls of the Potomac River, upstream from Washington, D. C. and cascading between Maryland and Virginia shores, is shown here as depicted in 1802, in an engraving by T. Cartwright after a drawing by G. Beck, London. Courtesy of the Library of Congress

Built c. 1738 by Thomas Lee, Stratford was home to his eight children, two of whom, Richard Henry Lee and Francis Lightfoot Lee, were signers of the Declaration of Independence. A distant cousin, Robert E. Lee, was born there in 1807. Courtesy of the Robert E. Lee Memorial Foundation

Born in 1720 in Scotland, John Carlyle became a prosperous merchant and married Sarah, the daughter of William Fairfax of Belvoir. He built the grandest mansion in town, Carlyle House, completed in 1752. Here the colonial governors met with British Gen. Edward Braddock in 1755 to coordinate action against the French and Indians. Photograph courtesy of the Northern Virginia Park Authority

The building of the Mount Vernon mansion was done gradually, beginning with Lawrence Washington's modest little cottage to which George Washington made additions. He connected the main house and its principal dependencies with colonnade-covered walkways. Courtesy of the Mount Vernon Ladies' Association of the Union

Artist Edward Savage painted George Washington's family at Mount Vernon in 1790. With the couple are Martha's grandchildren, George Washington Parke Custis and Eleanor Parke Custis. The African-American servant on the right is William Lee. Courtesy of the National Gallery of Art

Gunston Hall was the home of George Mason. Architect William Buckland completed the design in 1758. The property was given to the Virginia Commonwealth by Louis Hertle in 1932. It is administered and exhibited by the National Society of Colonial Dames. Dennis McWaters photo of the riverfront facade of Gunston Hall courtesy of Gunston Hall Plantation

Blenheim was built on Old Lee Highway in the town of Fairfax about 1850 for Captain Rezin Willcoxin. During the Civil War, it was occupied by Union troops who left legible graffiti on the attic walls – names, addresses, and sketches. The City of Fairfax bought the building in 1999 to make it a museum. Courtesy of the Fairfax Museum and Visitors Center

There is a celebratory air about Alexandria's Market Square when the weekly Saturday market is held and merchants and customers come together to enjoy the experience. This is believed to be the oldest continuous Saturday market in the nation. The City Hall appears in the background. It was constructed in 1871. The earlier Fairfax County Courthouse stood on this square from 1752 until 1800. Courtesy of the artist, Jackie Cawley

Seen beyond the colorful foliage of Occoquan Regional Park is the Occoquan River, bordered on the far shore by the town of Occoquan, which was chartered in 1804. Large flour and cotton mills were operated there by the Ellicott and Janney families. Photograph by W. B. Folsom, courtesy of the Northern Virginia Regional Park Authority

Native of Virginia *was painted around 1925 by Gari Melchers. The model was Mrs. Annie DeShields of Garrisonville, in Stafford County. In 1931 the painting was awarded the Maryland Art Institute Gold Medal. Oil on canvas.* Courtesy of Belmont, the Gari Melchers Estate and Memorial Gallery, Mary Washington College, Fredericksburg, Virginia

The Hunters *is one of Gari Melchers' later paintings. Falmouth and the Rappahonnock River are shown in the background. Oil on canvas.* Courtesy of Belmont, the Gari Melchers' Estate and Memorial Gallery, Mary Washington College, Fredericksburg, Virginia

This Lovettsville postman preferred a sulky to an RFD wagon. Photo taken in July 1911, colored by artist Elsie E. Lower, courtesy of the National Archives

This is the view of Main Street in the City of Fairfax facing east from Fairfax Courthouse hill as it appeared in the early twentieth century. The old Fairfax Herald *newspaper office and the 1901 Town Hall are on the left.* Courtesy of the artist, Ellen Jones

Welbourne is an eighteenth century stone house which became the home of the Dulany family in 1819. Colonel Richard Henry Dulany founded the Upperville Union Club, the forerunner of the Upperville Colt and Horse Show. He was the late nineteenth century Master of the Piedmont Foxhounds, whose 1966 counterparts are shown in front of the mansion. Courtesy of the photographer, Howard O. Allen

The 1,000-acre estate Morven Park, near Leesburg, was purchased in 1903 by Westmoreland Davis, who became governor of Virginia in 1918. It is owned and administered by The Westmoreland Davis Memorial Foundation, Inc., established by Mrs. Marguerite Davis in 1954. Housed on the estate are the governor's mansion, a carriage collection assembled by Viola Townsend Winmill and the Museum of Hounds and Hunting. Morven Park Mansion photgraph courtesy of the Westmoreland Davis Foundation, Inc.

The only known example of an American "scurry," a stylized type of hunt painting made up of portraits of the participants based on 18th century British traditions, was painted by Jean Bowman in 1988. Among the notable riders are Senator John Warner and Jacqueline Kennedy Onassis, widow of President John F. Kennedy. Organized in Orange County, New York in 1900, the Orange County Hunt moved to Fauquier County in 1903. Courtesy of the Museum of Hounds and Hunting

The Commonwealth Foxhounds are shown moving away from the mansion at Ingleside Plantation at Opening Meet on the first Saturday in November. Astride the horses in the foreground are Master of Foxhounds Robert M. Hoyer, who organized the hunt in 1981, and Dr. Eugene Guazzo, who has blessed the hounds. Built in 1833, Ingleside has been home since 1890 to the Flemer family, who operate a winery and other horticultural activities here and on several adjoining estates in Westmoreland County. Courtesy of Mr. and Mrs. Robert M. Hoyer, Co-Masters of Foxhounds

The bronze statue of Mercury atop a twisted column of Carrara marble at Reston Town Center's Fountain Square, designed by sculptor Saint Clair Cemin, was augmented by a new gleaming pavilion with bones of steel and a skin of glass in 1993. The pavilion accommodates summer concerts, winter skating, parties, weddings and other activities.
Courtesy of Reston Land Corporation

This regatta at Sandy Run Regional Park is illustrative of the many water-related sports available at the parks and waterways of Northern Virginia. Photograph by Carol Ann Cohen, courtesy of the Northern Virginia Regional Park Authority.

The Udvar-Hazy Center of the National Air and Space Museum at Dulles Airport houses exhibits from the Smithsonian Institution's aircraft collection in a hanger-like building covering the length of three football fields, and standing ten stories high at the top of its arched ceiling. Photo courtesy of Ross Netherton

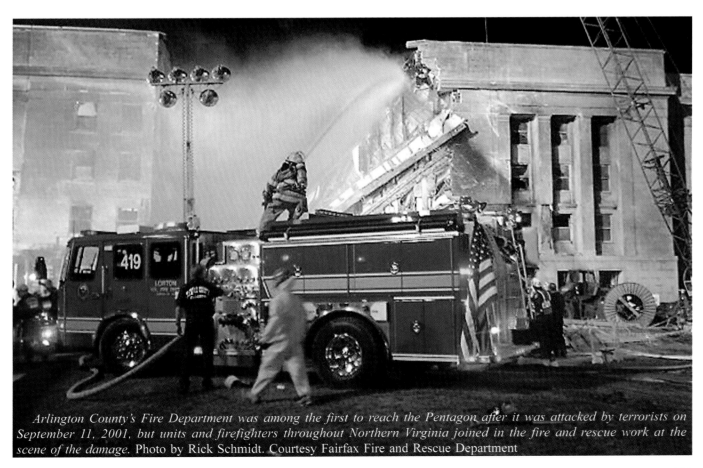

Arlington County's Fire Department was among the first to reach the Pentagon after it was attacked by terrorists on September 11, 2001, but units and firefighters throughout Northern Virginia joined in the fire and rescue work at the scene of the damage. Photo by Rick Schmidt. Courtesy Fairfax Fire and Rescue Department

St. Mary's Catholic Church at Fairfax Station was built in 1858 for Irish immigrants and local Catholics. During the Civil War, Clara Barton, founder of the American Red Cross, tended wounded soldiers here. Many of those who died were buried nearby. From an oil painting by Gerald Hennesy

Occoquan was chartered by the Virginia state legislature in 1804 and large flour and cotton mills were established by the Ellicott and Janney families. In recent years the Prince William Marina has served boating enthusiasts and the little town has become a popular arts and crafts retail center. Courtesy of the artist, Jackie Cawley

A Selected List of Sources

Arlington Historical Society, *Arlington*. Charleston: Arcadia Publishing, 2000

Cox, Ethelyn, *Historic Alexandria, Street by Street*. Alexandria: Historic Alexandria Foundation, 1976

Clark, W. M. ed., *Colonial Churches*, Richmond: Southern Churchman Co., 1907

Dawe, Louise Belote, *Christ Church*, revised edition. Irvington: Foundation for Historic Christ Church, Inc., 1985

Evans, D'Anne, *Prince William County, A Pictorial History*. Norfolk: the Donning Company, 1989

Fairfax County, Virginia, Clerk of the Courts, *Registration of Free Negroes, 1822 – 1861*, 1977

Ibrahim, Karen King, et. al., *Fauquier County, Virginia Register of Free Negroes, 1817 – 1865*. Midland, Va.: Afro-American Historical Association of Fauquier County, 3rd edition, 1993

Fithian, Philip V., *Journal and Letters of Philip Vickers Fithian, 1733 – 1774*, edited by Hunter Dickinson Farish. Charlottesville: The University Press of Virginia, 1943

Fitzhugh, William, *William Fitzhugh and His Chesapeake World*, edited by Richard Beale Davis. Chapel Hill: the University of North Carolina Press, 1968

Garrreau, Joel, *Edge City: Life On The New Frontier*. New York: Doubleday, 1991

Gottmann, Jean, *Virginia In Our Century*, new printing. Charlottesville: The University Press of Virginia, 1969

Handbooks, Inc, *Loudoun Handbook*, 1998 edition. Bridgewater, Va.: Good Printers, 1998

Harper, Robert R., *Richmond County, Virginia, A Tricentennial Portrait*. Alexandria: O'Donnell Publications, 1992.

Harrison, Fairfax, *Landmarks of Old Prince William County*, vols. I & II, 2nd reprint edition. Baltimore: Gateway Press, Inc., 1987

Harrison, Noel Garraux, *City of Canvas: Camp Russell A. Alger and the Spanish-American War*. Falls Church: Falls Church Historical Commission and Fairfax County History Commission, 1988

Head, James W., *History and Comprehensive Description of Loudoun County, Virginia*. Park View Press, 1908

Hening, William Waller, *Statutes of Virginia – Being a Collection of All the Laws of Virginia From the First Session of the Legislature in the Year 1619*. Richmond: J and G. Cochrane Printer, 1821

Harwell, Richard Barksdale, ed., *The Committee of Safety of Westmoreland and Fincastle*. Richmond, The Virginia State Library, 1956.

Hiden, Martha W., How *Justice Grew: Virginia Counties, an Abstract of Their Formation*. 3rd printing. Charlottesville: The University Press of Virginia, 1980

Jones, Stewart, et al., *Foundation Stones of Stafford, Virginia*, Vols. I and II. Fredericksburg: The Fredericksburg Press, Inc., 1991, 1992

Kirby, Jack Temple, *Westmoreland Davis, Virginia Planter – Politician, 1859 – 1942*. Charlottesville, The University Press of Virginia, 1968

Lossing, Benson I., *Mount Vernon and Its Associations*, New York: John C. Yorston & Company, 1859

Loth, Calder, ed., *The Virginia Landmarks Register*, 3rd edition. Charlottesville: The University Press of Virginia, 1986

Moore, Fay Montague, *Seaport in Virginia, George Washington's Alexandria*. Charlottesville: The University Press of Virginia, 1949

Netherton, Nan and Ross, *Arlington County in Virginia, A Pictorial History*. Norfolk: The Donning Company, 1986.

Netherton, Ross and Nan, *Fairfax County, A Contemporary Portrait*. Norfolk: The Donning Company, 1992

Netherton, Nan and Ross, *Fairfax County in Virginia, A Pictorial History*. Norfolk: The Donning Company, 1986

Netherton, Nan et al., *Fairfax County, Virginia, A History*. Fairfax: Fairfax County Board of Supervisors, 1978

Norris, Walter Briscoe, Jr., *Westmoreland County, Virginia, 1653 – 1985*. Montross: Westmoreland County Board of Supervisors, 1983

O'Neal, William B., *Architecture in Virginia*. New York: Walker & Company, Inc., for the Virginia Museum, 1968

Potter, Stephen R., *Commoners, Tribute, and Chiefs, The Development of Algonquin Culture in the Potomac Valley*. Charlottesville: The University Press of Virginia, 1994

Prince William, A Past To Preserve. Prince William County Historical Commission, 1982.

Reid, Frances H., *Inside Loudoun: The Way It Was*. Leesburg: The Loudoun Times-Mirror, 1986

Reniers, Perceval, *The Springs of Virginia: Life, Love, and Death at the Waters, 1775 – 1900*. Chapel Hill: University of North Carolina Press, 1941

Ryland, Elizabeth Lowell, *Richmond County Virginia*. Warsaw: Richmond County Board of Supervisors, 1976

Salmon, Emily J. and Campbell, Edward D. C., Jr., eds., *The Hornbook of Virginia History*, 4th ed. Richmond: the Library of Virginia, 1994

Simmons, Catherine T., *Manassas, Virginia, 1873 – 1973*. Edited by Douglas K. Harvey. Manassas, Va., : The Manassas City Museum, 1986

Smith, William Francis and Miller, T. Michael, *Seaport Saga, Portrait of Old Alexandria, Virginia*. Norfolk: The Donning Company, 1989

Smoot, Betty Carter McGuire, *Days In An Old Town*. Alexandria: Privately Printed, 1934.

Templeman, Eleanor Lee and Netherton, Nan, *Northern Virginia Heritage*. New York: Avenel Books, 1966

Virginia Writers Program, *Virginia, A Guide to the Old Dominion*. New York: Oxford University Press, 1940

Waterman, Thomas Tileson, *The Mansions of Virginia, 1706 – 1776*. New York: Bonanza Books, 1945

Willis, Barbara Pratt and Felder, Paula S., *Handbook of Historic Fredericksburg, Virginia*. Fredericksburg: Historic Fredericksburg, Virginia Foundation, Inc., 1987

Wilson, Donald L., "William Grayson and the American Constitution," *Word From the Junction* (The Manassas City Museum News) [periodical] June 1988

Wilson, John C., *Virginia's Northern Neck*, A Pictorial History. The Donning Company, 1984

Wrenn, Tony P., *Falls Church, History of a Virginia Village*. Falls Church: Falls Church Historical Commission, 1972.

Index

1 Hunting Creek Bridge to Mount Vernon 2 Fort Lyons
3 Fort Ellsworth 4 Fairfax Seminary 5 Pa Reserves
6 Government Bak ... y 7 Orange & Alexandria R R Depot.
8 Provost Marshals Office.

BIRDS EYE VIEW

Published by Chas Magnus 1...